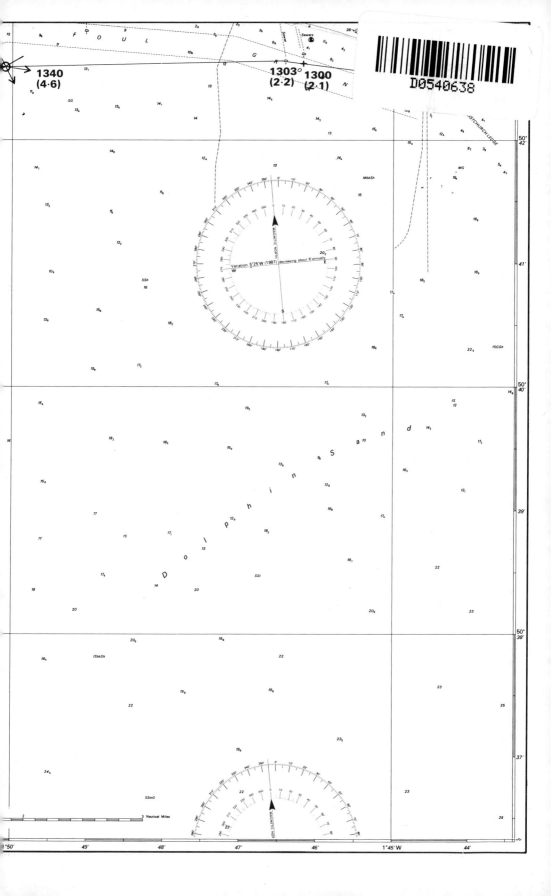

DAY SKIPPER

Other books for RYA courses

Day Skipper Exercises
Pat Langley-Price & Philip Ouvry
ISBN 0 7136 4630 6
A companion to *Day Skipper, Day Skipper Exercises* is packed with question papers on chartwork, tides, pilotage and passage planning and so provides ideal practice for all students completing the RYA Day Skipper shorebased course or for revision prior to commencing Coastal Skipper or Yachtmaster Offshore courses. It includes practice chart 5061 and relevant notes and tide tables so that the questions can be completed without reference to other publications.

RYA Book of Navigation
Tim Bartlett
ISBN 0 7136 4409 5
The reference text for anyone following RYA Navigation courses from Day Skipper through to Yachtmaster Offshore.

The RYA Book of Navigation Exercises
Alison Noice & James Stevens
ISBN 0 7136 4644 6
Written by the RYA staff who actually compile the test papers, *The RYA Book of Navigation Exercises* provides practice questions and answers at both Day Skipper and Coastal Skipper/ Yachtmaster levels.

Yachtmaster
2nd edition
Pat Langley-Price and Philip Ouvry
ISBN 0 7136 3772 2
This very popular course manual covers the whole of the shorebased syllabus of the RYA/DTp Yachtmaster Offshore Certificate, plus extra material on specialised topics. There are Test Papers and exercises at the end of each chapter, all of which are based on Admiralty Instructional Chart No 5055 which is supplied with *Yachtmaster Exercises*.

Yachtmaster Exercises
2nd edition
Pat Langley-Price and Philip Ouvry
ISBN 0 7136 3810 9
This companion volume to *Yachtmaster* is packed with practice exercises and answers, including over 50 model plots. Use it to polish up before the exam or in classroom exercises. It comes complete with a full sized Admiralty Instructional Chart 5055.

Ocean Yachtmaster
Revised edition
Pat Langley-Price and Philip Ouvry
ISBN 0 7136 4553 9
The ideal classroom course textbook for the thousands who embark each year on the most advanced RYA/DTp grade – the Yachtmaster Ocean Certificate. Using this book and its exercises the student will be able to study from home.

Ocean Yachtmaster Exercises
Pat Langley-Price and Philip Ouvry
ISBN 0 7136 4830 9
Companion volume to *Ocean Yachtmaster* for those taking the Yachtmaster Ocean Certificate and for navigators' revision.

Ocean Navigator
6th edition
Kenneth Wilkes
Revised by Pat Langley-Price and Philip Ouvry
ISBN 0 7136 3924 5
It contains everything the ocean navigator needs to work out sight reductions for the sun, the moon, the four navigable planets, the fifty-seven selected stars, and Polaris. With *Ocean Navigator* on board, a navigator has all he needs to make a passage across any of the world's oceans.

VHF Yachtmaster
2nd edition
Pass Your Exam the Easy Way
Pat Langley Price and Philip Ouvry
ISBN 0 7136 3786 2
This textbook and its accompanying cassette have been produced as a complete self-tutor for the aspiring operator who wishes to become a fluent radio communicator. It includes all the information necessary to pass the examination.

DAY SKIPPER

· including pilotage and navigation ·

Second Edition · Revised

**Pat Langley-Price
and Philip Ouvry**

ADLARD COLES NAUTICAL
London

Published by Adlard Coles Nautical
an imprint of A & C Black (Publishers) Ltd
37 Soho Square, London W1D 3QZ
www.adlardcoles.co.uk

First edition published by Adlard Coles 1988
Second edition published by Adlard Coles Nautical 1991
Reprinted 1993
Revised 1996
Reprinted 1998, 2000, 2001

ISBN 0 7136 6178 X

A CIP catalogue record for this book is available from the British Library

Typeset in Baskerville by CG Graphic Services, Aylesbury, Bucks
Printed and bound in Great Britain by MPG Books Ltd, Bodmin, Cornwall

Contents

Acknowledgements

The authors wish to thank the following: Helen Deaves of Stanford Charts; W. & H. China. Extracts from Admiralty tide tables are reproduced with the sanction of the Hydrographic Department, MOD. Extracts from the Convention on the International Regulations for Preventing Collision at Sea 1972 are reproduced courtesy of the International Maritime Organisation.

List of Plates

Introduction

'Classroom navigators are all very well,' said the principal of a practical sailing school, 'but they do seem to find it difficult to put theory into practice.' 'Why don't you write about pilotage: taking a boat in and out of harbours and around the coast with plenty of buoys and landmarks,' he continued, 'and while you are about it, explain how to read a chart: to recognise the buoys, beacons, lighthouses, headlands, chimneys, towers, transits, leading lines, clearing bearings and so on. Tell them about ropework, anchoring and, most important, safety. Make it suitable for motor boats as well, not just sailing boats.'

Having completed *Competent Crew*, which is *an introduction to practical sailing*, and having written *Yachtmaster*, which is *an examination handbook for students on Royal Yachting Association (RYA) courses*, it seemed appropriate to take up the points made by the sailing school principal with a book suitable for the explorer of creeks and estuaries, the local fisherman, the coast hugger, the motor boater and the trailer sailor, the learner, the less experienced . . . This is it: this is *Day Skipper*.

What have we done in *Day Skipper*? In Part 1 we have headed for the quiet backwaters of Poole Harbour and the adjoining coastline from Swanage to Christchurch. Very conveniently Stanfords produce a yachtsman's chart covering the area which includes a wealth of information on pilotage, weather forecasting and emergency procedures. All the exercises are set on this chart and a practice version is included with the book. We have added useful bits of information on different techniques and methods to cover completely the pilotage and navigation for the RYA Day Skipper qualification. We have included a full description of electronic navigation aids which are becoming inexpensive enough to be installed in many small craft. There are examples and exercises, with illustrations and fully worked answers. We have also included over 25 photographs to show how the symbols and views on the chart appear in practice. For anyone cruising around Poole it is almost a guidebook in itself; but we must not say *guidebook*, it's not nautical: it should be *pilot* or *sailing directions*.

In Part 2 there is a comprehensive list explaining nautical terms and definitions, with diagrams illustrating parts of the boat. Ropework and anchorwork are covered and we have explained the important Collision Rules concerning steering and sailing. Key features of personal and boat safety are included.

It has been hard work to produce and we hope you find it useful. Please let us know, through the publisher, if you have any suggestions or comments.

We do wish you happy and safe sailing; and safe navigation.

Revised edition

It is our policy to keep up to date the chart enclosed with this book. The end papers, however, are from an earlier edition of the chart. The main differences between the earlier edition and the present edition of the chart relate to a marine radiobeacon on the Haven Hotel and a sectored light marking the entrance to Poole harbour via the East Looe channel. The text has been altered, where it matters, to take account of the chart corrections.

Pat Langley-Price
Philip Ouvry

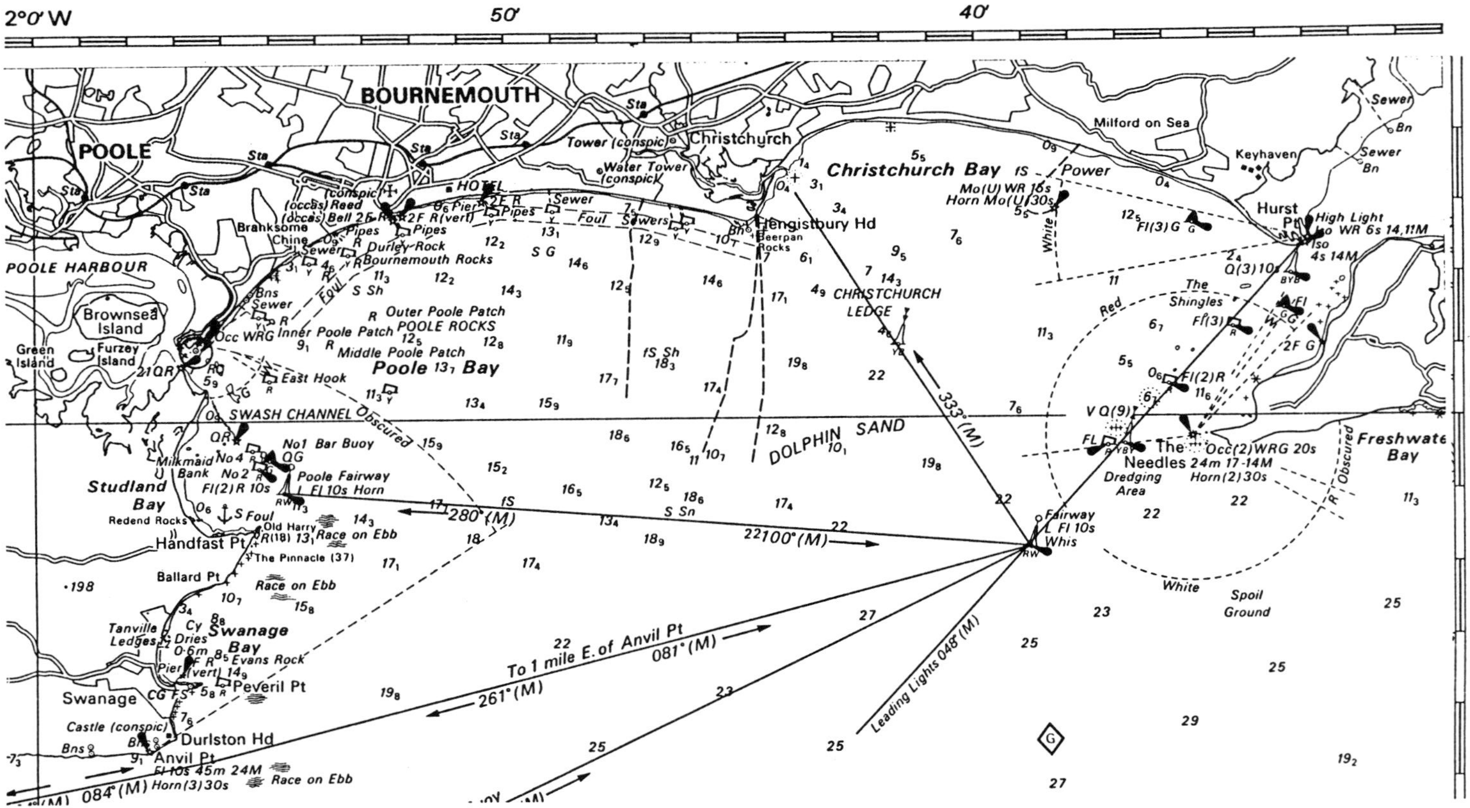

Fig 1.1 A portion of small scale chart 12 English Channel

PART 1

Chapter One

What is a Chart?

A chart is a seafarer's map. It is used like a map to identify: a position; a destination; and the best route between the two.

Fig 1.1 shows a portion of the chart which covers the area from Needles, Isle of Wight, to Start Point. The title is: *The English Channel from the Needles to Start Point* and the chart number is 12. It is a small-scale chart showing a large area but not much detail and is used for planning a sea passage. Now look at chart number 15 (provided) which covers the area from Durlston Bay to Christchurch Bay. It is of a larger scale than chart 12 (Fig 1.1) and contains much more detail. This type of chart is used when approaching a harbour or an anchorage as many of the features and hazards shown are omitted on a small-scale chart.

Refer to chart 15. The title and number of the chart are shown on the outside cover and repeated on the map side. Under the title there is an explanation of the symbols and abbreviations used together with navigational information. To the left, about half way down, are tables showing the direction and rate of the tidal streams at specific places. The chart is metric which means that all heights and depths are in metres. Distances are always in nautical miles, and speeds or rates are in knots, which are nautical miles per hour.

Fig 1.2 shows a compass rose which is used to define direction. It is graduated in degrees (°) from 0 through 360. There are three compass roses on chart 15.

The latitude scale is down each side of the chart and the longitude scale is along the top and bottom. These scales are used in the same way as a grid on a map to identify a specific position. The latitude scale is also used for measuring distance.

On the reverse side of the chart is information concerning navigation, pilotage, weather and safety.

In the next chapter the chart is explained in detail.

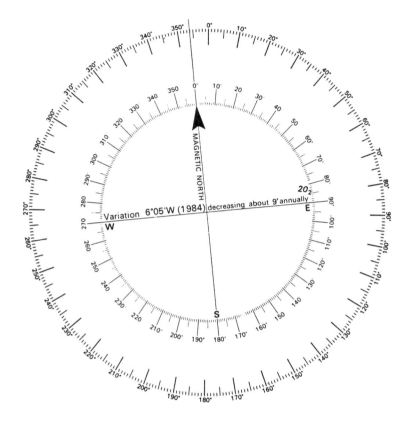

Fig 1.2 A compass rose

QUESTIONS

Use chart 15 to answer these questions.

1.1 What is the main difference between chart 15 and the portion of chart 12 (Fig 1.1)?

1.2 What is the title of chart 15?

1.3 What are the figures:
  a. down the side border of the chart;
  b. along the top and bottom of the chart?

1.4 How can a specific position be identified on chart 15?

1.5 What is a knot?

Chapter Two

How a Chart is Made

A chart is a representation of a portion of the earth's curved surface projected on to a flat area. There are several ways of doing this but the main type of projection used on navigational charts is called **Mercator**.

Fig 2.1a represents the earth, overlaid with imaginary lines of latitude and longitude. Lines of latitude (known as parallels of latitude) are equally spaced either side of the Equator. Latitude is 0° at the Equator, increasing to 90° at each pole. Lines of longitude (known as meridians) converge at the North and South Poles. The meridian passing through Greenwich, London, is the datum meridian for longitude. Longitude is 0° at Greenwich increasing to 180° east and west of the Greenwich meridian.

Fig 2.1b represents a mercator projection chart. Parallels of latitude and meridians of longitude appear as parallel lines at right angles to each other. To allow for the east–west distortion caused by this projection, the parallels of latitude are spaced increasingly further apart as the distance from the Equator increases. On this form of projection a straight line representing the track of a vessel crosses all meridians at the same angle. Such a line is known as a **Rhumb Line**. Because of the distortion of this projection, mercator charts cannot be used either for polar regions (latitudes greater than 70°) or for passages in excess of 600 nautical miles. The charts in these cases use a **Gnomonic** projection which has the advantage that a straight line on the chart represents the shortest distance on the earth's surface. For convenience, large-scale charts, such as chart 15, use a gnomonic projection; though for navigational purposes they can be used as a mercator projection.

Both latitude and longitude scales are divided into units called degrees (°) with sub-divisions into minutes (') and tenths of a minute. There are 60 minutes in one degree. Sixty degrees ten point five minutes would be written: 60° 10'.5. Like a grid, coordinates from both scales are used to identify a position. The latitude scale is also used for measuring distance because one minute of latitude is equivalent to one nautical

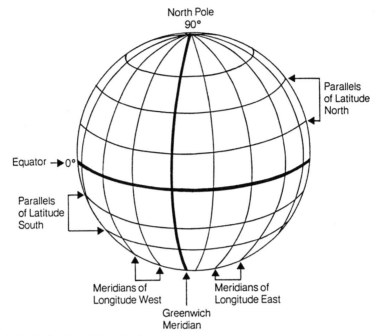

Fig 2.1a Latitude and longitude

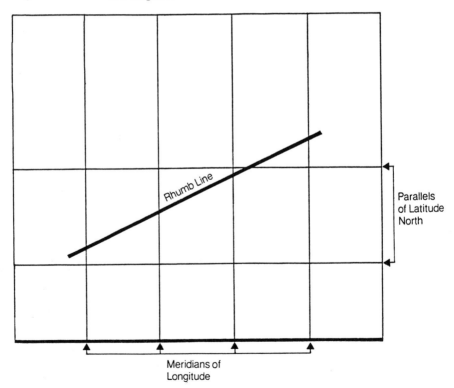

Fig 2.1b Mercator projection

mile (M). (A nautical mile – 6076 feet or 1852 metres – is not equal
to a statute mile – 5280 feet.) With mercator projection, as latitude
increases the scale increases, so distance must *always* be measured from
the latitude scale level with the boat's position (Fig 2.2).

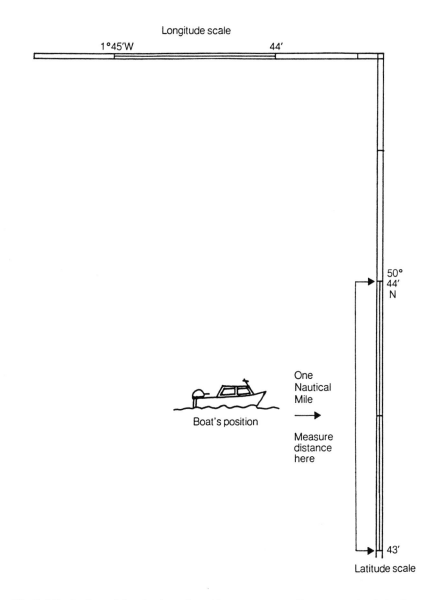

Fig 2.2 Latitude and longitude scales. Always measure distance on the latitude
scale level with boat's position

QUESTIONS

2.1   Why is it important to measure distance from the latitude scale in the area of the boat's position?

2.2   What are the properties of a mercator projection chart?

2.3   Why is it not possible to use mercator projection charts for polar regions and for passages over 600M?

2.4   What is the datum meridian for longitude?

2.5   How would you write in figures: Fifty degrees, thirty-eight point five minutes?

Chapter Three

Using a Chart

Refer to chart 15.

To measure on a chart latitude, longitude, direction and distance the normal navigational instruments used are a parallel rule and dividers. These instruments are used in the explanations in this book. Other navigational instruments (such as Douglas and Portland protractors, Breton and Hurst plotters) are often more convenient on a small boat; and they are supplied with a full set of instructions.

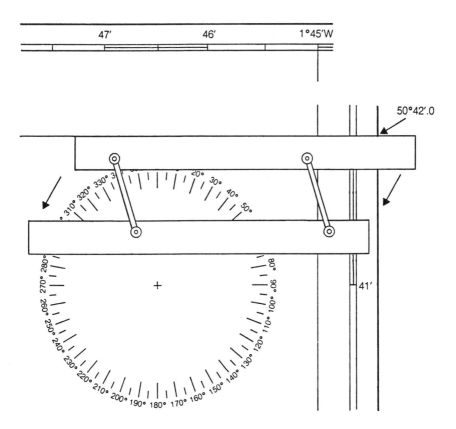

Fig 3.1a Measuring latitude

To measure latitude

Look at the compass rose at the top right-hand corner of the chart. To find the latitude of the centre point of this compass rose, place the closed parallel rule along the parallel of latitude nearest to the compass rose, 50° 42'.0. Keeping a firm hold on the top half of the rule, move the bottom half until the bevelled edge passes through the centre point, Fig 3.1a. It will intersect the latitude scale to the right of the compass rose, Fig 3.1b. The figure on the scale through which it passes is 50° 41'.0. The latitude of the centre point of the compass rose is 50° 41'.0N: north (N) because the latitude is north of the Equator.

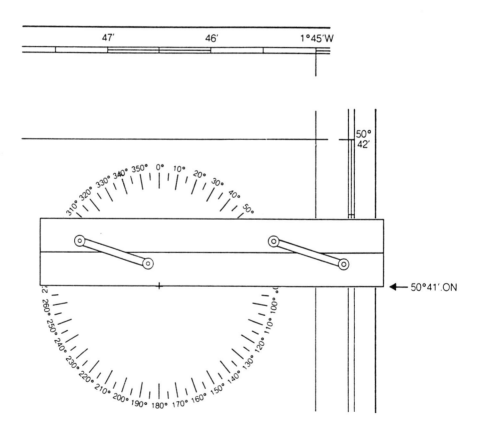

Fig 3.1b Measuring latitude

To measure longitude

To find the longitude of the centre point of the same compass rose, place the closed parallel rule along the meridian of longitude to the right of the compass rose, 1° 45'.0, Fig 3.2a. Move each half of the parallel rule alternately across the chart (known as 'walking' the rule) so that the edge passes through the centre point. It will intersect the longitude scale at 1° 46'.5, Fig 3.2b. The longitude of the centre point of the compass rose is 1° 46'.5W: west (W) because the longitude is west of the Greenwich meridian.

Now use the dividers on the meridian to the right of the compass rose (1° 45'W) and the other point at the centre of the compass rose, Fig 3.3. Keeping the dividers this distance apart, transfer them to the top

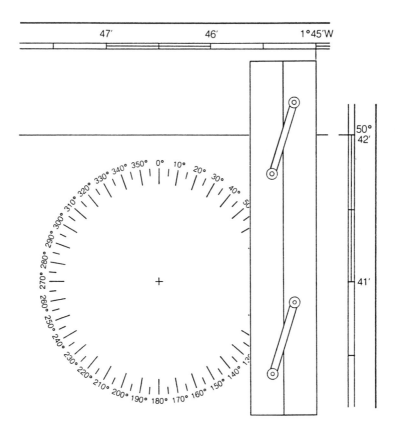

Fig 3.2a Measuring longitude

longitude scale. One point will be at the intersection of the meridian; the other will be on the figure 1° 46′.5. The longitude at the centre of the compass rose is 1° 46′.5W. So the longitude found by using the dividers corresponds with that found using the parallel rule (Fig 3.2b). Similarly latitude can also be found using dividers. In practice the parallel rule and dividers are used together: one for latitude and the other for longitude.

Recording a position

When recording a position, latitude is written first followed by longitude; 50° 41′.0N 1° 46′.5W.

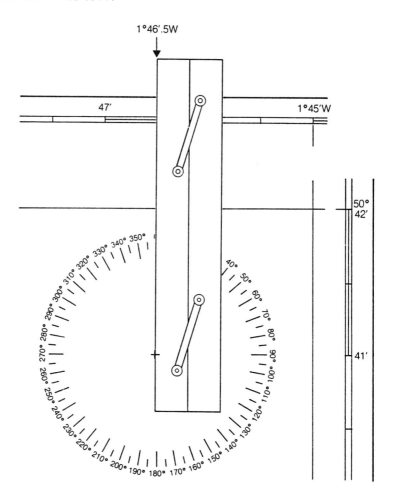

Fig 3.2b Measuring longitude

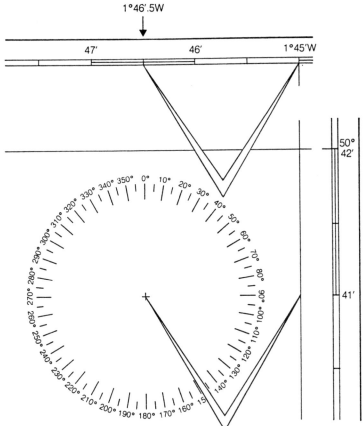

Fig 3.3 Using dividers to measure longitude

Plotting a position

Now plot position 50° 41'.5N 1° 45'.5W. This is the reverse of the previous procedure. Place the parallel rule along the meridian nearest to 1° 45'.5W: this is 1° 45'.0W. Walk it to the right until the edge intersects the longitude scale at 1° 45'.5W. Leave the parallel rule in this position. Use the dividers to mark off the latitude. Place one point on the latitude scale on the parallel nearest to 50° 41'.5N: this is 50° 42'.0N. Place the other point on 50° 41'.5N. Keeping the dividers this distance apart, move them to the parallel rule with one point on the parallel 50° 42'.0N. The other point will be on the required latitude of 50° 41'.5N. Mark the position, Fig. 3.4.

Finding direction

Examine the compass rose (Fig 1.2). This consists of two circles both graduated through 360°. For the moment we are only concerned with

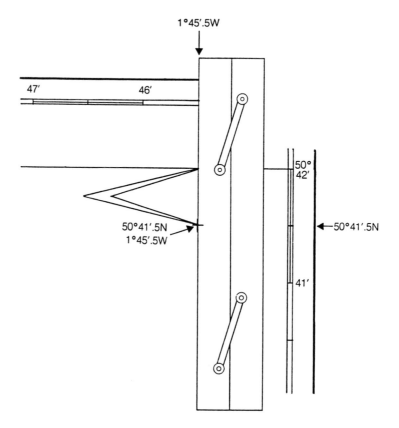

Fig 3.4 Plotting a position

the outer circle. Place the parallel rule across the compass rose so that the edge passes through the centre and the figures 0° and 180°, Fig 3.5a. The figure 0° represents the direction of geographical north (called true north) and the figure 180° is the direction of south. Direction is measured clockwise from true north through 360°.

Place the parallel rule with its edge across the centre and through the figures 90° and 270°, Fig 3.5b. The rule is now in an east–west direction in line with the parallels of latitude, 90° is east and 270° is west.

Now imagine that you are standing at the centre point of the compass rose looking out in the direction of the figure 40°, Fig 3.6. A line drawn from the figure 40° to your position would, if extended, pass through the figure 220°. The same line can indicate two directions. Walk forward towards the figure 40°: you are now travelling in the direction of 40°. For clarity, the directions round the compass rose are abbreviated. In practice directions are given using a three figure notation, so 40° would

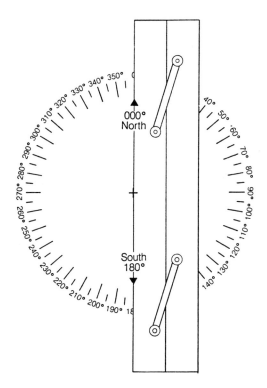

Fig 3.5a Direction – north and south

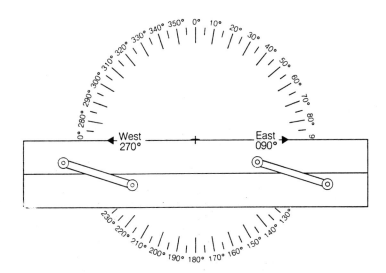

Fig 3.5b Direction – east and west

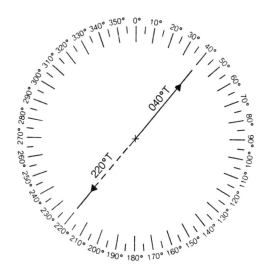

Fig 3.6 Finding direction

be written 040°. We have used true north as our reference point so we can indicate this by putting the letter 'T' after the figures; so 040° becomes 040°T. The direction behind us is known as the reciprocal direction and always differs by 180°: it is 220°T. A boat pointing in the direction of 040°T is on a course (or heading) of 040°T.

Suppose we are in a boat in a position 50° 42'.5N 1° 47'.0W and we wish to find the direction of the beacon at the end of the groyne off Hengistbury Head (50° 42'.6N 1° 44'.9W). Align the edge of the parallel rule between the boat's position and the beacon, Fig 3.7. Walk the parallel rule so that the edge passes through the centre of the nearest compass rose. It will pass through the figures 85° and 265°. The beacon at the end of the groyne off Hengistbury Head from the boat's position is in the direction of 085°T. It is said to be on a bearing of 085°T. From the beacon the bearing of the boat is 265°T, this being the reciprocal of the bearing 085°T. A reciprocal bearing is always 180° different from the original bearing.

If the parallel rule is a Captain Fields pattern engraved with a protractor scale, Plate 1, it is not necessary to walk it across the chart to the compass rose. There is an easier way. For example, from the position 50° 42'.8N 1° 49'.0W, we wish to know the bearing of Boscombe Pier (50° 43'.1N 1° 50'.5W). Place the edge of the parallel rule between our position and Boscombe Pier, Fig 3.8.

Walk the rule to the nearest meridian so that the intersection of the

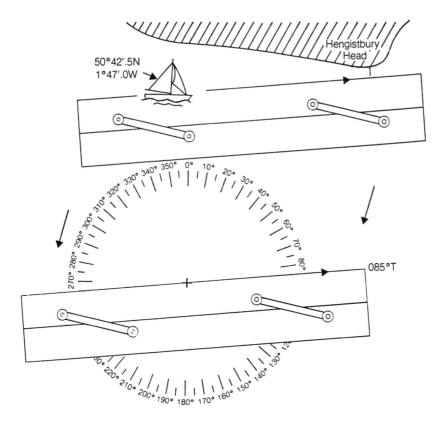

Fig 3.7 Using the compass rose to find direction

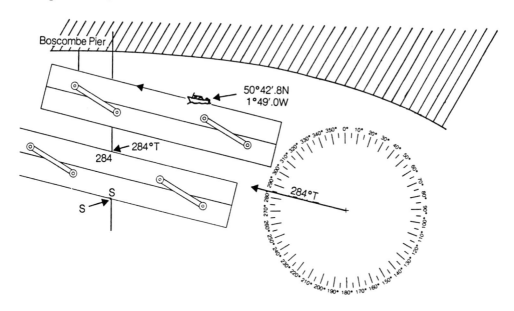

Fig 3.8 Using a parallel rule to find direction

S (south) line and the edge of the rule is *exactly* on the meridian. Close the other part of the rule. Follow the meridian up from this point of intersection to the scale and read off the figures. We have two figures, one of which is the reciprocal of the other. If you are not sure which is correct, imagine you are at the centre of the compass rose looking outward. In this case the bearing of Boscombe Pier from our position is 284°T.

Wind directions are always given as the direction *from which* the wind is blowing using the compass point notation rather than the 360° notation, Fig 3.9.

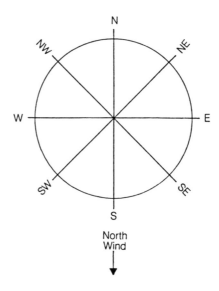

Fig 3.9 A north wind blows *from* the north

Measuring distance

Distance is measured in nautical miles. By definition one nautical mile is equivalent to one minute of latitude. Distance is always measured on the latitude scale level with the area concerned. (On a large-scale chart, such as chart 15, there is occasionally a mean distance scale. This is not included on a small-scale chart.)

To measure the distance from the centre of the compass rose (50° 41'.0N 1° 46'.5W) to the beacon at the end of the groyne off Hengistbury Head, open out the dividers putting one point on each of the two positions. Keeping the dividers at the same distance apart, transfer them to the latitude scale alongside, Fig 3.10. They span one complete graduation and 0.95 of the next. As one graduation (one minute of latitude) is equivalent to one nautical mile, the distance from the centre

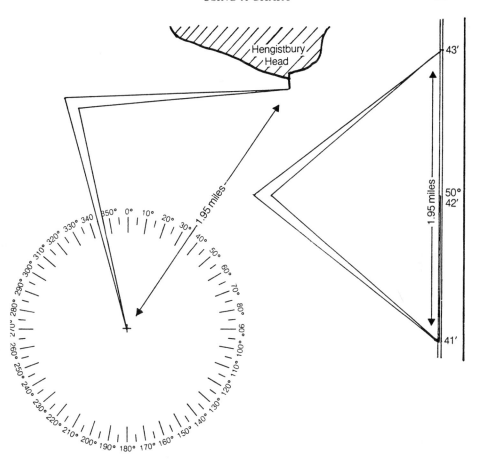

Fig 3.10 Measuring distance

of the compass rose to the beacon is 1.95 nautical miles (or 1.95M). In practice we only work to the nearest tenth of a nautical mile, so we would write 2.0M.

Now measure the distance between the centres of the compass roses in positions 50° 36′.3N 1° 46′.5W and 50° 40′.0N 1° 53′.1W. The dividers are too small to span this distance. Open the dividers to a convenient distance, say 2.0M, and 'walk' them from one position towards the other, Fig 3.11.

After two spans the distance remaining is less than 2.0M. Set the dividers to this remaining distance and measure it off on the latitude scale: it is 1.6M. The total distance is 5.6M (2.0 + 2.0 + 1.6).

To measure a given distance from a position, set the distance on the dividers using the latitude scale (level with the required area) then place one point of the dividers on that position and the other in the given direction.

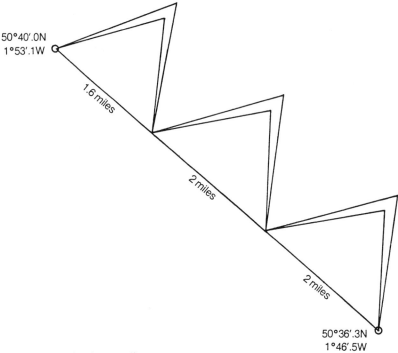

Fig 3.11 Measuring longer distances

To draw a straight line between two positions at opposite ends of a large chart, it is often convenient to fold over the edge of the chart so that it passes through both positions. The edge can now be used to draw the line.

Defining a position

A position is defined either by its latitude and longitude or by its bearing and distance *from* a known landmark. A position of 50° 42′.8N 1° 49′.0W could also be defined as 104°T *from* Boscombe Pier 1.0M.

QUESTIONS

3.1   Plot a position 50° 35′.5N 1° 57′.5W. What is in this position?

3.2   Draw a line from a position 0.2M south of the beacon at the end of the groyne off Hengistbury Head to a position 0.2M south of the pierhead at Boscombe.
a. How close does this line pass to the yellow buoy which is 1M from the groyne?
b. How close does the line pass to the yellow buoy off Boscombe Pier?

3.3a. What is the true direction of Bournemouth Pier from Handfast Point?

b. What is the distance from Handfast Point to Bournemouth Pier?

c. How long would it take a boat travelling at 4.5 knots to cover this distance?

3.4   Plot a position 218°T from Bournemouth pierhead 2.9M.

3.5   What is the latitude and longitude of a position 111°T from the flagstaff (*FS*) on Peveril Point 1.1M? (*Note:* The flagstaff is in position 50° 36'.4N 1° 56'.6W.)

Chapter Four

What Affects the Compass?

Variation

In Chapter Three we ignored the inner circle on the compass rose. The inner circle is the magnetic compass rose. A compass needle points towards magnetic north, not towards true or geographic north. The magnetic north pole is about 1000 nautical miles from the geographical North Pole: it is situated in the area of Hudson Bay, Canada. In practice to find direction we use a compass which contains a needle shaped magnet suspended so that it is free to rotate horizontally. This magnet rotates until it points towards magnetic north. Normally directions on the chart are relative to true north (as shown on the outer circle of the compass rose). The angular difference between true north and magnetic north is called **Variation**, Fig 4.1.

The variation depends on geographical position and can be as much as 30° in certain areas of the world where small craft are likely to go. Because the magnetic pole rotates slowly around the geographical North Pole, there is also a slight change every year in any one geographical position. When navigating we frequently measure direction using a magnetic compass. Before this magnetic direction is plotted on the chart it is converted to true. We are constantly correcting between magnetic bearings and courses and true bearings and courses; see Chapter Ten.

The variation, and the year to which it applies, is printed on a chart across the compass rose. Look at the compass rose in position 50° 41'.0N 1° 46'.5W: the variation is 4° 30'W (1995) decreasing about 7' annually. However, at the compass rose in position 50° 36'.3N 1° 46'.5W the variation is 3° 55'W. As we tend to use variation corrected to the nearest degree, there is only likely to be a significant change of variation in voyages over 200 nautical miles.

In Poole Bay the variation is 4° 30'W in 1995 decreasing about 7' annually. In 1998 it will have decreased by 21', so it will be 4° 09'W. In practice we would correct this to the nearest whole degree: 4° W.

We need to remember whether to add or subtract variation when we

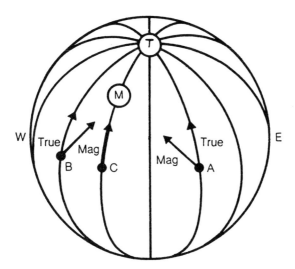

Fig 4.1 Variation – Magnetic north M is offset slightly from true north T, so the variation between the two will depend on where you are on the earth's surface in relation to them. At point B variation is East, at A it is West, while at C the variation is nil since true and magnetic north are directly in line

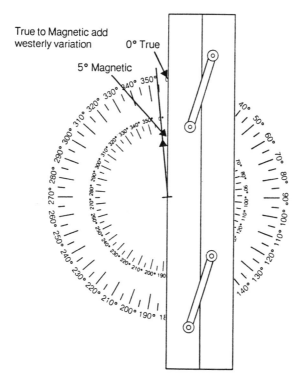

Fig 4.2 Applying variation

are working between magnetic and true directions. Here is a way to remember. Refer to Fig 4.2. Place the parallel rule on the compass rose so that it passes through the figures 0°T and 180°T. The rule crosses the magnetic rose at 005°M (M for magnetic). So the magnetic direction is 5° greater than the true direction. The deflection is to the left or west. So we have a simple rule:

True to magnetic *add* variation west

Magnetic to true *subtract* variation west

Example 1a

True course	265°T	Magnetic course	148°M
Variation	+ 5°W	Variation	– 7°W
Magnetic course	270°M	True course	141°T

To indicate a magnetic course or bearing, the letter 'M' is placed after the figures. For variation east the rule is opposite to that for variation west:

True to magnetic *subtract* variation east

Magnetic to true *add* variation east

Example 1b

True course	111°T	Magnetic course	344°M
Variation	– 3°E	Variation	+ 5°E
Magnetic course	108°M	True course	349°T

Deviation

A compass can also be affected by the close proximity of ferrous metal, electrical circuits and electronic equipment containing magnets. All of these produce influences that may cause the compass magnet to deflect from magnetic north. Any such deflection is called **deviation**.

The compass used by the helmsman is known as the **steering compass**. It is in a fixed position.

The site of the steering compass is important: the compass **heading** (the direction in which the boat is pointing) must be clearly visible to the helmsman; it must be firmly secured and in a safe position where it will not be damaged in heavy weather or by clumsy crew members; it should be well away from any deflecting influences; and the **lubber line** (the mark on the fixed part of the compass indicating the heading) must be accurately aligned with the fore-and-aft line of the boat.

For such a compass it is possible to compensate partly for any permanent magnetic influence by the location of magnetised needles adjacent to the compass; but this is a specialised task carried out by a qualified compass adjuster. The adjuster will manoeuvre the boat round in a circle measuring at regularly spaced headings the deviation of the steering compass: this procedure is known as a **compass swing**. Any remaining deviation will be tabulated for each compass heading in a **deviation table**. If the compass is re-sited, another compass swing is necessary. Deviation alters with a change of heading of the boat, so a deviation table will show the deviation to be applied for different headings of the boat, Fig 4.3. Deviation can be either east or west of magnetic north and corrections are applied using the same rules as for variation.

Compass Heading	Deviation
000°	5°E
020°	5°E
040°	4½°E
060°	4°E
080°	3½°E
100°	1½°W
120°	2½°W
140°	4°W
160°	5°W
180°	4½°W
200°	3½°W
220°	2°W
240°	0°
260°	2½°E
280°	4°E
300°	4½°E
320°	5°E
340°	5°E

Fig 4.3 Deviation table

A compass reading that has not been corrected for deviation or variation is shown by placing the letter 'C' after the figures.

Example 2a

Compass course	141°C	True course	057°T
Deviation	– 4° W	Variation	+ 6° W
Magnetic course	137°M	Magnetic course	063°M
Variation	– 5° W	Deviation	– 4°E
True course	132°T	Compass course	059°C

Compass error

If variation and deviation are aggregated together, the result is known as **compass error**.

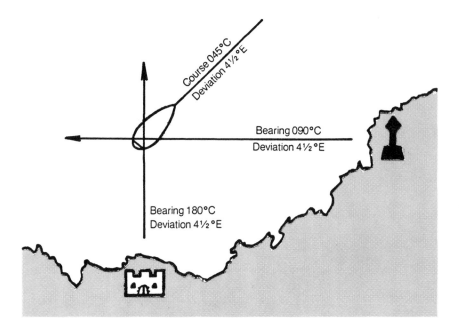

Fig 4.4 Deviation changes with the boat's heading, not with the bearings taken whilst on that heading. Thus if the deviation on heading 045°C is 4½E, the deviation remains 4½E for all bearings taken with the steering compass whilst on that heading.

Example 2b

Variation	6°W	True course	057°T
Deviation	– 4°E	Compass error	+ 2°W
Compass error	2°W	Compass course	059°C

Hand-bearing compass

For taking bearings of landmarks, buoys and other vessels in the vicinity a separate hand-held compass is used. As it is not fitted in a permanent position, there can be no deviation table for it so it must be used in positions on a boat where there is negligible deviation. Any bearings taken with a hand-bearing compass are magnetic bearings.

If the course indicated on the steering compass is suspect, it can be checked against the direction of the boat's head using the hand-bearing compass. With the boat on a steady course, the hand-bearing compass is lined up with the fore-and-aft line of the boat and the readings of the two compasses compared.

Example 3

Steering compass	340°C
Hand-bearing compass	346°M
Deviation	6°E

QUESTIONS

4.1 What is the variation in Poole Bay in position 50° 40′N 1°55′W for the year 1999?

4.2a. Correct the following true bearings to magnetic bearings:

Bearing	Variation
218°T	6°W
147°T	4°E
359°T	10°W

  b. Correct the following magnetic bearings to true bearings:

Bearing	Variation
001°M	9°W
178°M	7°E
007°M	5°E

4.3a. Correct the following magnetic bearings to compass bearings:

Bearing	Deviation
010°M	9°E
356°M	8°W
162°M	4°E

  b. Correct the following compass bearings to magnetic bearings:

Bearing	Deviation
241°C	10°W
054°C	12°E
292°C	3°W

4.4 A boat is on a course of 060°C. The variation is 6°W; the deviation is shown in Fig 4.3. The following bearings are taken using the steering compass:

Tower	091°C
Church	167°C
Monument	330°C

  a. What are the true bearings to plot?
  b. What is the compass error?

4.5 What should be taken into consideration when siting a compass?

Chapter Five

Reading the Shorthand

Chart symbols

In order to include navigational information on the chart but still leave it legible, many symbols and abbreviations are used. Some of these are self-explanatory, Fig 5.1; but others need interpretation, Fig 5.2.

Telephone   Yacht club

Fig 5.1   Fig 5.2

Whilst a key may be included on some charts, generally it is necessary to refer to another publication such as *Symbols and Abbreviations used on Admiralty Charts*, which is Admiralty chart 5011 published in booklet form.

On chart 15 under the title there is an explanation of some of the symbols and abbreviations used. See if you can find the symbols shown in Fig 5.3.

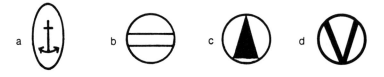

a   b   c   d

Fig 5.3

The symbols in Fig 5.3 are: Harbour office; Customs office; Marina; Visitor's berth.

Buoys are indicated by a small symbol showing their shape with letters to define their colour, Fig 5.4. Any light is shown by a magenta blob, Fig 5.5; the light characteristics being listed adjacent to the buoy symbol. The characteristics state: the number of times in a period that the light flashes or occults (goes out); the colour; and the length of the period, Fig 5.6.

Symbol	Description	Position on Stanfords Chart 15
 G	Green conical shaped buoy	50°39'.8N 1°55'.3W

Fig 5.4

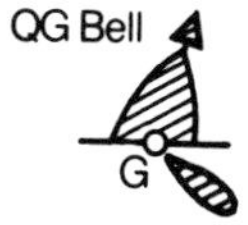

Symbol	Description	Position on Stanfords Chart 15
QG Bell G	Green conical shaped buoy with a conical shaped topmark, a green quick flashing light and a bell	50°39'.4N 1°55'.1W

Fig 5.5

Symbol	Description	Position on Stanfords Chart 15
Fl R 2s	Red can shaped buoy with a can shaped top mark and a red light showing one flash every 2 seconds	50°39'.2N 1°55'.2W

Fig 5.6

The positions of lighthouses and lights on land used for navigation are shown by a star augmented by the magenta blob, Fig 5.7. For these, additional information on sectored lights, height of light, luminous range of the light and fog signalling apparatus is included.

Symbol	Description	Position on Stanfords Chart 15
 Fl 10s 45m 24M	Lighthouse with a white light flashing every 10 seconds. It is 45 metres high. The light is visible for 24 miles.	50°35'.5N 1°57'.5W

Fig 5.7

Some heights of easily identifiable or conspicuous (*conspic*) landmarks (churches, towers, chimneys, radio masts) are given, Fig 5.8. Such heights are shown in brackets, e.g. (21), and are in metres above a datum level called **mean high water springs** (MHWS) which is defined in Chapter Six.

In anchorages the quality of the sea-bed is indicated, Fig 5.9.

Depths of water (below the datum level of the chart) are shown in metres and tenths of a metre, Fig 5.10. A **drying height**, which is the height to which a rock or sandbank would be exposed if the sea level fell to the datum level of the chart, has the same basic abbreviation as a charted depth but, in addition, the number indicating metres is underlined, Fig 5.11.

Tidal stream data is keyed to a specific position using a tidal diamond, Fig 5.12.

Symbol	Description	Position on Stanfords Chart 15
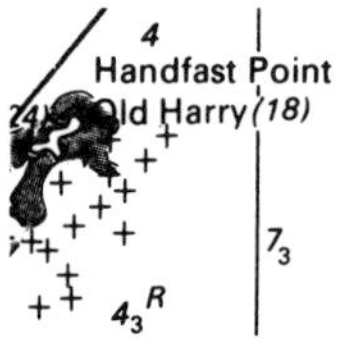	Old Harry rock is 18 metres above MHWS	50°38′5N 1°55′.3W

Fig 5.8

fS Sm St bk Sh	Fine sand, small stones, broken shells	50°38′.7N 1°55′.4W

Fig 5.9

16_4	Depth below chart datum (16.4 metres)	50°41′.7N 1°44′.2W

Fig 5.10

$\underline{0}_7$	Drying height (0.7 metres)	50°38′.9N 1°56.9W

Fig 5.11

 B	Tidal diamond	50°39′.2N 1°54′.9W

Fig 5.12

Chart corrections

As well as keeping a chart up-to-date, it is important to be able to know that a chart has been fully corrected. Commercial publishers from time to time issue a list of corrections, or a chart can be returned for updating. However, the trend is to re-issue a chart at regular intervals.

Corrections to Admiralty charts are promulgated in a weekly bulletin known as the *Admiralty Notices to Mariners (weekly edition)*. Each Notice lists all the charts (and publications) affected, together with the number of the Notice with the last correction. When a correction is made, the year and number of the Notice are noted in the bottom left-hand corner of the chart. If the last correction was not shown, then it could be incorporated. For United Kingdom waters a 'small craft' edition of the *Admiralty Notices to Mariners* is published (four times a year) which only includes corrections to home waters charts.

QUESTIONS

5.1 What publication shows chart symbols and abbreviations?

5.2a. Using chart 15, identify the following:

1   2   3

b. What chart symbols are in the following positions:
   50° 40'.5N   50° 38'.7N   50° 43'.4N
   1° 56'.1W   1° 55'.8W   1°47'.9W
   c. What is the quality of the bottom in position 50° 38'.7N 1° 55'.8W?

5.3 Draw a line from 50° 38'.7N 1° 56'.0W to No 8 red buoy south east of Training Bank. What is the minimum charted depth along this line?

5.4 What is the significance of the wavy lines in position 50° 35'.3N 1° 56'.5W?

5.5 What is the height of Anvil Point light?

Chapter Six

What Causes the Tides?

Tides are vertical movements of water caused by combinations of the gravitational pull of the sun and the moon.

Each day around the British Isles there are normally two high tides, when the sea-level reaches its highest point, called high water (HW), and two low tides when the sea-level is at its lowest point, called low water (LW). A rising tide (flood tide) is the period between LW and HW, and a falling tide (ebb tide) the period from HW to LW. The height difference between HW and the preceding or succeeding LW is called the **range**; and the time difference is called the **duration**. The difference from HW or LW to any given time is known as the **interval**. The depth of water shown on a chart (the **charted depth** or **sounding**) is the depth of the seabed below the chart datum which is the lowest level to which the tide is expected to fall due to astronomical conditions (**Lowest Astronomical Tide** or **LAT**).

The tide level does not rise and fall by the same amount each day. Over a period of approximately two weeks the heights of high water and low water vary from a minimum to a maximum then back to a minimum. The combination of the highest high water and the lowest low water (maximum range) is called a **spring** tide; and the combination of the lowest high water and the highest low water (minimum range) a **neap** tide, Fig 6.1. During one four-week period there will be two spring tides and two neap tides.

At the time of the equinoxes (21st March and 23rd September) when the earth and the sun are closest together, the spring tides have the greatest range and are known as **equinoctial spring tides**.

The height of a tide can be affected by weather conditions. If the barometric pressure is high (1040mb) over a period of several days, the increased pressure of the air on the sea surface can lower the sea-level by as much as 0.3 metres. A strong wind blowing into an estuary over a period of several days can raise the sea-level by a similar amount; or

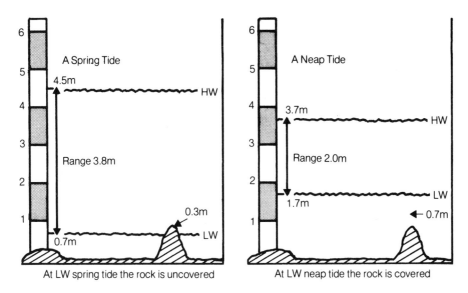

Fig 6.1 Spring and neap tides

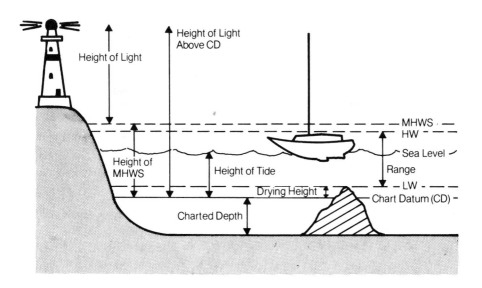

Fig 6.2 Datum levels

conversely lower it if the wind is blowing out to sea. Under these circumstances variations in predicted heights and times of high and low water can occur.

Datum levels

We have defined **chart datum** or **CD** as the lowest level to which the tide is expected to fall due to astronomical conditions. Other datum levels are shown in Fig 6.2. They are all 'mean' (average) levels taken over a period of one year: mean high water springs (MHWS) being the mean height above chart datum of the high waters of spring tides. Mean high water springs (MHWS) is used as the datum level for heights of land features. For comparison with the heights of land features shown on maps, large-scale charts and tide tables include the differences between chart datum and the Ordnance Survey datum for various locations.

QUESTIONS

6.1   What is chart datum?

6.2   Can the tide ever fall below chart datum?

6.3a.   What is charted depth?
    b.   How is this shown on chart 15?

6.4   What datum level is used when indicating the height of land features?

6.5   When does the greatest range of tide occur?

Chapter Seven

How Much Water is There?

Information on tides is found in *Admiralty Tide Tables*, a yachtsman's almanac or local tide tables. There are tables which show the times and heights of high water and low water at main ports (called **standard ports**). For other ports, known as **secondary ports**, the times and heights of high water and low water are found by corrections to the adjacent standard port times and heights. These corrections, known as **secondary port differences**, are found in a separate set of tables. Some local tide tables incorporate these differences.

The tables only give the height of the tide at the time of high water and low water. To find out the height of tide at other times, diagrams of **tidal curves** are used. There are tidal curves for each standard port; and, with certain exceptions, the same tidal curves are used for the associated secondary ports.

To understand how to use the tide tables and tidal curves we will work through some examples. All heights are in metres and all times are indicated using a four-figure notation based on a 24 hour day. Times shown are in local mean time (UK: GMT). During summer months 1 hour must be added (UK: BST).

Standard ports

To find the time for a given height of tide at a standard port.
Use Extract 1 p. 188 for Examples 4 and 5.

Example 4
At what time (BST) at Dover during the afternoon of 2nd June will the tide rise to a height of 3.2m?
For the period covering the afternoon of 2nd June, extract from the tide tables for the port of Dover the times and heights of high water (HW) and low water (LW) and work out the range by subtracting the height of LW from the height of HW. Convert all times to BST.

	LW Time	Height	HW Time	Height	Range
Dover	0915 GMT	1.6	1427 GMT	5.8	4.2
Add 1 hour	+ 0100		+ 0100		
Dover	1015 BST		1527 BST		

Refer to the tidal curve diagram, Fig 7.1.
1. Fill in on the time scale at the bottom of the tidal curve diagram the time of HW (1527) and hours before and after HW as required.
2. Mark the height of HW (5.8) on the top height scale (H.W.Hts.m) and the height of LW (1.6) on the bottom height scale (L.W.Hts.m).
3. Draw the range line between the HW mark and the LW mark.
4. Mark the height of tide required (3.2) on the top height scale and draw a line vertically downwards to the range line.
5. From the point of intersection on the range line draw a horizontal line to the right to cut the rising or falling curve as appropriate. It may be necessary to interpolate between the curves for spring and neap ranges. Compare the range (4.2) with the mean ranges shown in the top right-hand corner of the tidal curve diagram: springs 5.9m, neaps 3.3m . In this case the range (4.2) is halfway (0.5) between the mean ranges for springs and neaps. (Draw a line vertically downwards from the tidal curve to the time scale and read off the interval: HW–2h 50m. Apply this interval to the time of HW to give the time required of 1237.

(*Note:* An interval is shown as before or after HW by the use of a – or + sign.)

To find the height of tide at a given time at a standard port.

Example 5
What will be the height of tide at Dover on 17th May at 1100 BST?
For the period including 1100 on 17th May, extract the times and heights of high water and low water from the tide tables for Dover and work out the range.

	LW Time	Height	HW Time	Height	Range
Dover	0833 GMT	0.9	1341 GMT	6.2	5.3
Add 1 hour	+ 0100		+ 0100		(0.2 from
Dover	0933 BST		1441 BST		springs)

Refer to the tidal curve diagram, Fig 7.2.

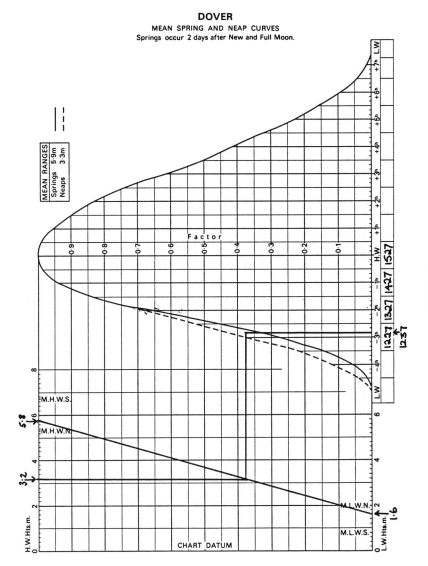

DOVER
MEAN SPRING AND NEAP CURVES
Springs occur 2 days after New and Full Moon.

Fig 7.1

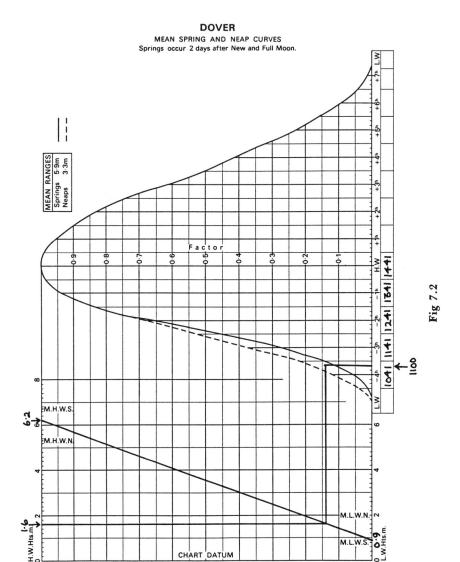

DOVER
MEAN SPRING AND NEAP CURVES
Springs occur 2 days after New and Full Moon.

Fig 7.2

Proceed as for Example 4 as far as step 3.

4. Enter the time scale with the interval HW–3h 41m (1100) and draw a line vertically upwards to the tidal curve interpolating if necessary between the spring and neap curves.
5. From this point on the tidal curve, draw a horizontal line to the left to the range line.
6. From the point of intersection on the range line draw a line vertically upwards to the height scale and read off the height which is 1.6m.

(*Note:* Although we have extracted the time of LW, it is not required in any calculation so it can be ignored.)

Secondary ports

HW and LW times and heights for secondary ports are obtained by applying secondary port differences to standard port tabulations (*refer to Extract 2*).

Suppose it is required to find HW at Folkestone at 0100 GMT. A difference of –20m is tabulated for Dover HW times of 0000 and 1200, and a difference of –5m for 0600 and 1800. The time interval between the tabulated time of 0000 and the required time of 0100 is 1 hour. The duration of the tide between 0000 and 0600 is 6 hours. 0100 is one-sixth of the duration. The range of the difference between –20m and –5m is 15m. The correction to apply to the Dover HW time will be one-sixth of the range of the difference, (2.5) applied to -20m = 17.5m. HW at Folkestone will be 0042 GMT.

$$\frac{\text{interval from HW}}{\text{duration of tide}} \times \text{range of difference} = \text{proportion of difference}$$

$$1/6 \times 15 = 2.5$$

Proportion of difference applied to tabulated figure:

$$20 - 2.5 = 17.5 \text{ (minus)}$$

It can also be done graphically (*see Fig 7.3*).

To find the time that the tide will reach a given height at a secondary port.
Use Extracts 1 and 2 p. 188 for Examples 6 and 7

Example 6
At what time (BST) will the tide first fall to a height of 2.5m at Ramsgate on 16th May?
For the period covering the falling tide on 16th May, extract the times

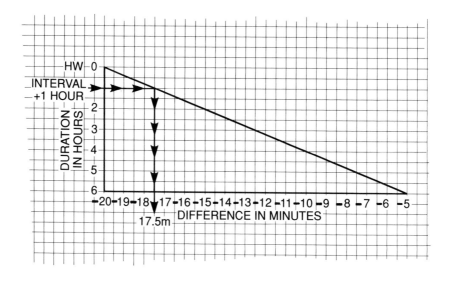

Fig 7.3 Secondary port differences

and heights of high water and low water at the standard port, Dover.
From the tide tables work out the range, then apply the tidal differences
for the secondary port, Ramsgate.

	HW		LW		
	Time	Height	Time	Height	Range
Dover	0017 GMT	6.4	0745 GMT	0.8	5.6
Differences	+ 0020	−1.8	−0007	−0.4	(nearly
Ramsgate	0037 GMT	4.6	0738 GMT	0.4	springs)
Add 1 hour	+ 0100		+ 0100		
Ramsgate	0137 BST		0838 BST		

Refer to the tidal curve diagram, Fig 7.4
The tidal curve diagram for the standard port is used as in Examples
4 and 5 but the times and heights of HW and LW at the secondary port
are entered on the diagram. The range at the *standard* port is required
for the interpolation between the spring and neap curves. The interval
is HW + 3h 30m. The time required is 0507. The time correction to
BST is made *after* the differences for the secondary port have been applied.

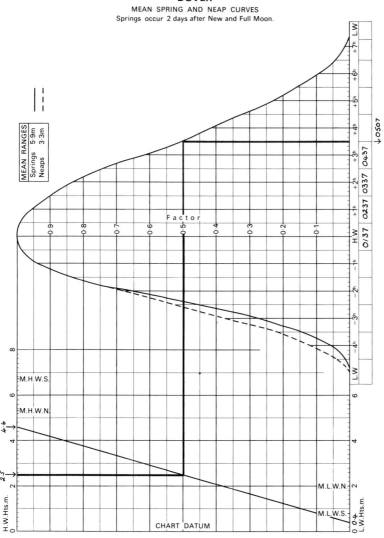

DOVER

MEAN SPRING AND NEAP CURVES
Springs occur 2 days after New and Full Moon.

Fig 7.4

To find the height of tide at a given time at a secondary port.

Example 7
What will be the height of tide at Folkestone on 4th June at 0930 BST?

	HW		LW		
	Time	Height	Time	Height	Range
Dover	0342 GMT	5.2	1041 GMT	2.0	3.2
Differences	– 0011	+ 0.4	– 0010	0.0	(neaps)
Folkestone	0331 GMT	5.6	1031 GMT	2.0	
Add 1 hour	+ 0100		+ 0100		
Folkestone	0431 BST		1131 BST		

Refer to tidal curve diagram, Fig 7.5.
Height required: 2.8m.

Solent ports (Swanage to Selsey)

Look at Fig 7.6 which is the tidal curve diagram for Lymington and Yarmouth, both of which come under the special classification of Solent ports. What are the differences between this diagram and the tidal curve diagram for Dover, Fig 7.1? There are two differences: Lymington and Yarmouth are both secondary ports, the standard port for the area being Portsmouth; and the time intervals are from LW not HW.

In the area covered by the Solent ports the tides are complex with the result that HW can remain at a steady level (called a stand of the tide) or occasionally fall a little then rise again for a second HW. The tidal pattern varies considerably between ports adjacent to each other. Therefore it is much easier to determine the time of LW rather than HW and so tidal curve diagrams use LW as the datum. As the tidal patterns of the secondary ports are so different to the standard port, Portsmouth, and to each other, a complete series of tidal curve diagrams is necessary. Poole Harbour, though not formally a standard port, has its own set of tide tables.

A slightly modified procedure is used with the tidal curve diagram for Solent ports.

To find the time for a given height of tide at a Solent port.

Use Extracts 3 and 4 pp. 189–90 for Examples 8 and 9

Example 8
At what time in the afternoon of 1st May will the tide at Lymington fall to a height of 1.8m?
For the afternoon of 1st May, extract the time and height of low water and the height of high water for the standard port, Portsmouth, and apply the tidal differences from Lymington.

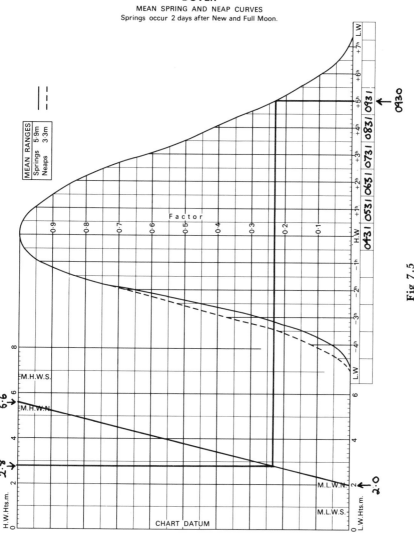

DOVER
MEAN SPRING AND NEAP CURVES
Springs occur 2 days after New and Full Moon.

Fig 7.5

| | HW | LW | | |
	Height	Time	Height	Range
Portsmouth	4.4	1827 GMT	1.1	3.3
Differences	− 1.5	− 0020	− 0.3	(mid range)
Lymington	2.9	1807 GMT	0.8	
Add 1 hour		+ 0100		
Lymington		1907 BST		

Refer to tidal curve diagram, Fig 7.6.
Fill in the time of LW and the heights of HW and LW. Compare the range on the tidal curve diagram to determine which curve to use. Proceed as for previous examples for secondary ports.

Interval: LW–1h 35m.
Time required: 1732.

To find the height of tide at a given time for a Solent port.

Example 9
What is the height of tide at Christchurch entrance on 16th July at 1140 BST?

| | LW | | HW | |
	Time	Height	Height	Range
Portsmouth	0815 GMT	0.8	4.7	3.9
Differences	− 0035	− 0.4	− 2.9	(springs)
Christchurch	0740 GMT	0.4	1.8	
Add 1 hour	+ 0100			
Christchurch	0840 BST			
Interval: LW + 3h 00m				

Refer to tidal curve diagram, Fig 7.7.
Height of tide required: 1.5m.

Clearances

With the knowledge of the height of tide at a particular location, examination of the depths of water and drying heights shown on the chart will enable the actual depth of water to be determined. If the draught of the boat is known, then the clearance between the bottom of the keel and the seabed can be worked out, Fig 7.8.

If the information on the chart is dubious or lacking, the depth determined from the echo-sounder or lead line can be used to estimate the charted depth. To allow for any rounding in the tidal calculations and for any abnormal weather conditions, a minimum clearance of 0.5m between the keel and the seabed is normally assumed.

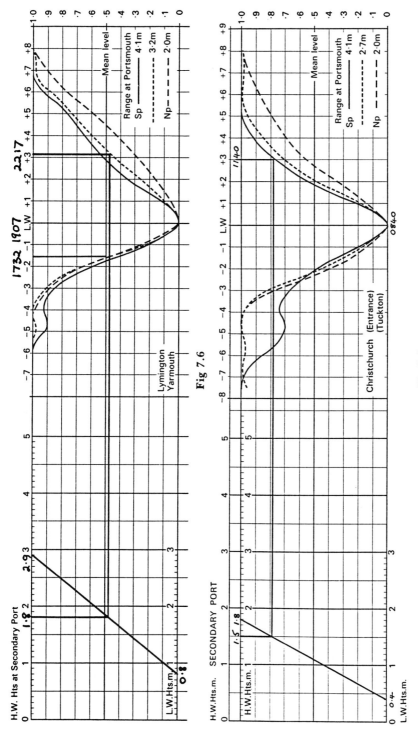

Fig 7.6

Fig 7.7

Example 10
A motor yacht whose draught is 1.1m anchors in the approaches to Lymington River at 1732 BST on 1st May. At that time the depth of water was 1.7m as measured on the echo-sounder which was sited 0.3m below the waterline. Will she be aground at low water; and how much anchor chain should she let out if she intends to remain overnight? Calm conditions are forecast.

Refer to Fig 7.8 and Example 8.

Example 8 shows that the height of tide at Lymington at 1732 on 1st May is 1.8m on a falling tide. LW is at 1907 and the height of tide at LW is 0.8m. If the echo-sounder is 0.3m below the waterline and indicates 1.7m, then the actual depth of water at 1732 is 2.0m. The seabed is therefore $2.0-1.8 = 0.2$m below chart datum (this means the charted depth would be shown as 0_2). The height of tide at LW is 0.8m above chart datum or $0.8 + 0.2 = 1.0$m above the seabed. As the motor yacht draws 1.1m, *she will be aground at LW*. At the following HW the height of tide will be 2.9m above chart datum or $2.9 + 0.2 = 3.1$m above the seabed. The rule of thumb to determine the length of anchor chain to let out is $4 \times$ maximum depth of water in calm weather or $4 \times 3.1 = 12.4$m; so 13m of anchor chain would be on the safe side.

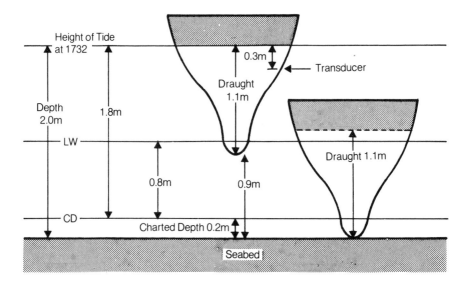

Fig 7.8 At 1732 the boat has a clearance above the sea bed of 0.9m but at LW she will be aground

Example 11
In Lymington River a boat goes aground on a falling tide at 1732 BST on 1st May. At what time might she expect to refloat?

Refer to Example 8 and tidal curve diagram, Fig 7.6.

In simple terms the question asks 'When will the height of tide return to the same level that it was at 1732'? On Fig 7.6 if the horizontal line is extended to the right to cut the mid range curve on the rising tide, and a line drawn vertically upwards, then this line will cut the time scale at LW + 3h 10m or 2217.

Example 12
In the morning of 16th July a motor yacht with a draught of 1.1m wishes to leave Christchurch harbour with a clearance of at least 0.5m over the bar at the entrance. What is the earliest time she can leave?

Refer to Example 9 and chart 15.

The inset on chart 15 for Christchurch harbour shows a depth over the bar at the entrance of 0.1m (0_1). The least depth of water required by the motor yacht is 1.1 + 0.5 = 1.6m. The height of tide required will be 1.6–0.1 =,1.5m. Example 9 shows that this height of tide will be reached at 1140 BST.

Heights of land features

All heights of land features are measured above the datum level of Mean High Water Springs (MHWS), Fig 6.2. Heights of features are in metres and are shown on the chart enclosed in brackets (18) (see Fig 5.8). The characteristics of lighthouses and lightships include the height of the light in metres above MHWS shown as a number followed by the letter 'm'. For Anvil Point light the characteristics are: Fl 10s 45m 24M. The height of the light is 45 metres above MHWS. The nominal range of the light is 24 nautical miles (24M). The **nominal range** of a light is the range at which it will be sighted when the normal meteorological visibility is 10M. It is really a measure of the brightness of the light.

Distance off when raising a light

The characteristics of a lighthouse show the height of the light above MHWS; which, for Anvil Point light, is 45m. The height of MHWS above chart datum can be determined from the tide datum levels shown on a chart. If the height of tide is also calculated, then the height of a light above sea level can be worked out. Tables can be found in yachtsmen's almanacs showing the 'distance off' of a light when it is first seen (or raised) on the horizon. To use these tables the observer must know his 'height of eye' above sea level; which, for a small craft, is usually 1.5m to 2.0m. For instance, at the time of high water, Anvil Point light would be raised from a boat with the height of the eye of the observer at 1.5m above sea level at a distance off of 16.5M.

See Extract 5 p. 190: Distance off a light

At night, particularly if the conditions are cloudy, the loom (reflected beam) of the light from a lighthouse can be seen considerably beyond the point at which the light itself becomes visible. Similarly the street lights of a port well over the horizon may appear as a dim glow in the sky.

QUESTIONS

For questions 7.3, 7.4, 7.5, use Extracts 1, 2, 3, 4 pp. 188–90 and Figs 7.1, 7.6

7.1   Where can information be obtained on times and heights of tides?

7.2   A boat with a draught of 2.0m needs a clearance of 0.5m to cross a sandbar which dries 1.3m. What is the height of tide required?

7.3   What is the height of tide at Dover on 17th June at 1920 BST?

7.4   At what time (BST) during the afternoon of 1st June will the tide first reach a height of 2.5m at Ramsgate?

7.5   What is the height of tide at Yarmouth at 1015 BST on 2nd June?

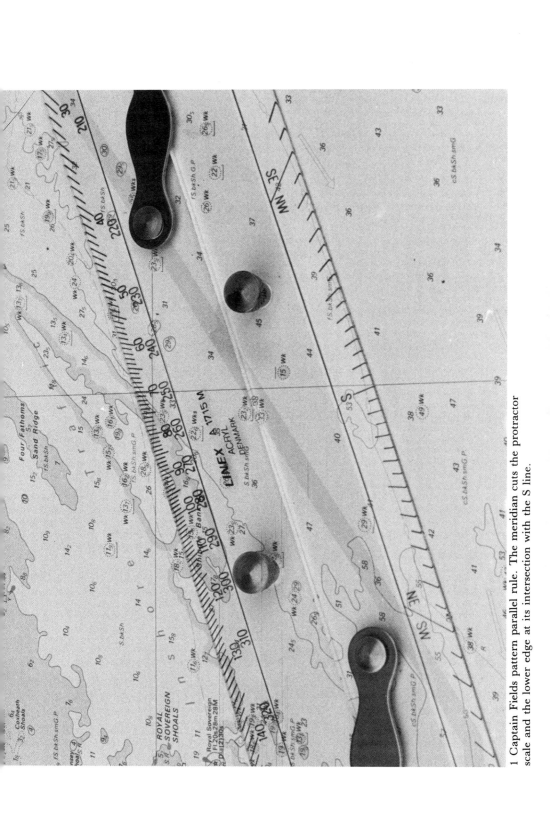

1 Captain Fields pattern parallel rule. The meridian cuts the protractor scale and the lower edge at its intersection with the S line.

Above: 2 Poole Fairway buoy marks the entrance to Poole. The training bank (outer end) beacon is visible on the port hand and the Haven Hotel in the distance. Buoy: safe water.

Below: 3 Leading line. Entrance to Beaulieu river showing leading line over the bar. The rear mark is occasionally obscured by the trees.

Right: 4 Christchurch Harbour entrance. The buoy is laid from May to October to indicate deep water over the bar. Buoy: port hand (secondary).

Above: 5 Groyne off Hengistbury Head. Red can-shaped beacon at southern end. Port hand beacon.

Below: 6 CG lookout – Hengistbury Head.

Above: 7 Christchurch Priory. View from a point to the west of Hengistbury Head. Buoy: yellow non-navigational.

Below: 8 Water tower (conspic). Becomes obscured by the cliff if the observer is closer to the shore.

Above: 9 Bournemouth – St Peter's church. St Peter's church is just open to the left of Bournemouth pier.
Left: 10 Bournemouth – hotel (conspic). Chine with beach below the hotel. Buoy: yellow non-navigational.
Below: 11 Poole Fairway – Handfast Point. Poole Fairway buoy is almost in transit with Handfast Point. Old Harry Rock is not clearly visible. Buoy: safe water.

Above: 12 Handfast Point – Durlston Head. Durlston Head is just open off Old Harry Rock.

Below: 13 Handfast Point. Old Harry Rock does not stand out. The anchorage in Studland Bay is visible beyond Old Harry's wife.

Above: 14 Peveril Ledge – Durlston Head. The castle is visible on Durlston Head. There are frequently extensive overfalls on the ebb tide around the buoy: port hand buoy.

Below: 15 Peveril Point. Ledge, Coastguard lookout and flagstaff on Peveril Point with castle on Durlston Head in background.

Above: 16 Swanage pier. Methodist church (with spire) and anchorage.

Below: 17 Swanage town. Transit of Methodist church and monument.

Right: 18 Anvil Point. Further to the north the lighthouse becomes obscured.

Above: 19 Ballard Point. Handfast Point in distance.

Below: 20 Haven Hotel.

Above: 21 East Looe channel. Inward
bound from East Looe buoy, leave the
N cardinal beacon to port and N
Haven Point about 100 yards to
starboard: port hand buoy.

Below: 22 Chain ferry. Note black ball
(lowered) on the ferry. The ferry
should be given a wide berth.

23 Bell buoy. Brownsea Road. The buoy marks the division between the Middle Ship channel to port and the North channel: south cardinal buoy.

Above: 24 Ro-Ro terminal. Power
station chimneys in background.

Below: 25 No. 67 Buoy. Off Poole Yacht
Club. Leading line beacons can be
seen on left hand side of picture
amongst small boat moorings:
starboard hand buoy.

Above: 26 No 76 Buoy. A line of port hand buoys across Wareham Lake leads to the River Frome. Buoy: port hand (secondary).

Below: 27 Poole Bridge. The lifting bridge in Poole town leading to Cobbs Quay and Holes Bay.

Chapter Eight

Tidal Stream: Fair or Foul?

The vertical rise and fall of the tide is the result of the horizontal movement of water known as a tidal stream. For specific positions on each chart there is a table which gives the true direction *towards* which the tidal stream is flowing together with the rate of flow in knots (nautical miles per hour) for both spring and neap tides. This information is tabulated for the time of high water at the associated standard port and at hourly intervals before and after. The specific positions are indicated by a diamond shape enclosing a letter: they are known as **tidal diamonds**, Fig 5.12.

Tidal stream diamonds

Refer to the tidal stream tabulation for tidal diamond B on chart 15. At HW (high water) the tidal stream at tidal diamond B will be setting in the direction 179°T at a rate of 0.8 knots for a spring tide and 0.4 knots for a neap tide. A boat travelling on a southerly course (180°T) would be assisted by this tidal stream which is said to be **fair**. For a boat travelling towards the north the passage time would be increased and this tidal stream is said to be **foul**. For a boat travelling east or west the tidal stream will be across the track and must be allowed for in determination of the course to steer. Later we will use the information from these tidal diamonds when we determine, by plotting on the chart, the effect of the tidal stream on the track of the boat.

For example, use tidal diamond B, HW Portsmouth 1300, springs. The direction and rate tabulated are mean values for one hour, so for the period from 0730 to 0830 the mean tidal stream would be 346°T 1.2k (HW−5). For the period from 0830 to 0930 the tidal stream would be 354°T 1.0k (HW−4). If, however, the tidal stream is required for the period from 0800 to 0900, then it would be necessary to use 30 minutes from the tidal stream tabulated for HW−5 (346°T 0.6M) and 30 minutes from that tabulated for HW−4 (354°T 0.5M).

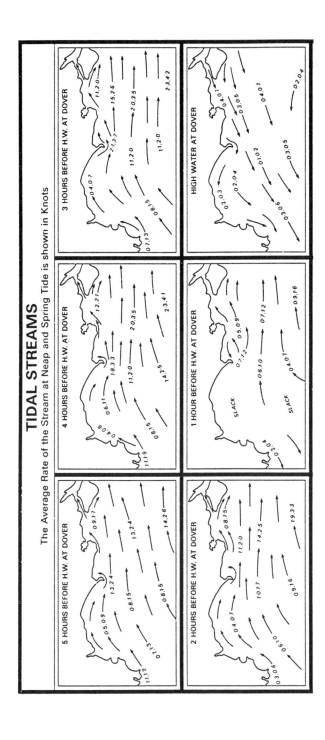

TIDAL STREAMS

The Average Rate of the Stream at Neap and Spring Tide is shown in Knots

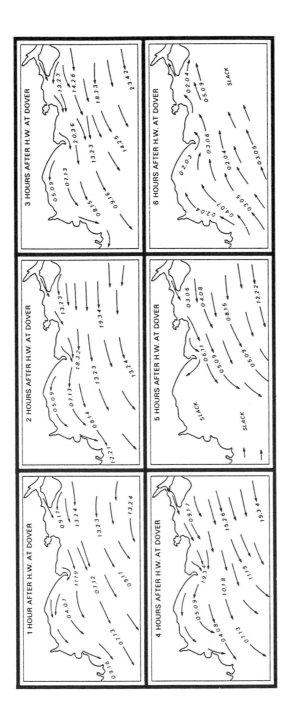

Fig 8.1

Tidal stream atlas

Tidal streams are also represented pictorially in a **tidal stream atlas** or **tidal stream diagram**, Fig 8.1.

Tidal stream atlases or diagrams are used either for passage planning or for pilotage. The arrow indicates the direction of flow. The figures are divided by the dot in the centre: the larger number representing the spring rate and the smaller the neap rate. (On Admiralty Tidal Stream Atlases the rates are multiplied by 10 for convenience: 12.24 is a neap rate of 1.2 knots and a spring rate of 2.4 knots.)

All the figures shown for rates of flow are mean rates; they can vary considerably at exceptional spring tides.

Effects of tidal streams

There is normally no tidal stream information for areas close inshore. Sometimes information on local effects is given in navigation guidebooks known as 'sailing directions' or 'pilots'.

Generally a tidal stream does not flow as strongly in shallow water; and in a bay it may sweep round in a contrary direction to the main

Fig 8.2 A good look at anchored vessels, buoys etc, will enable you to estimate the speed and direction of the tidal stream

stream. However, it tends to flow faster around headlands, sometimes causing severe tide races or overfalls where the water is very confused: see symbols on chart 15 in the vicinity of Durlston Head (50° 35'.6N 1° 57'.0W). It can also well up from an uneven bottom causing disturbed seas and eddies. These areas should be avoided particularly if the wind is blowing in the opposite direction to the tidal stream.

Every opportunity should be taken to observe the direction and rate of the tidal stream when passing moored boats, buoys and lobster pots, Fig 8.2.

In a river or tidal estuary the strongest current or tidal stream, and the deepest water, lie on the outside of a bend; the inside frequently silts up. In the absence of any buoys, beacons or withies, do not cut the corners on bends.

A tidal stream flowing over a shallow bank often produces a standing wave just downstream of the bank. Keep well clear of any such standing waves.

QUESTIONS

Use chart 15

8.1   What is the direction and rate of the tidal stream at spring tides one hour after high water in position 50° 39'N 1° 55'W?

8.2   In relation to high water when is the tidal stream east-going in the English Channel off Portland Bill (use Fig 8.1)?

8.3   At spring tides in the area covered by tidal diamond A, the tidal stream was flowing faster than tabulated. Why might this be?

8.4   The tidal stream at tidal diamond B is 026° 0.3k. The wind is from the west. The boats at anchor in Studland Bay are lying with their bows pointing west. Why?

8.5   Approaching Poole Fairway buoy, how can you check on the direction of the tidal stream?

Chapter Nine

Pilotage: Finding the Way Without Plotting

When making a short passage relatively close to the shore in good visibility, the navigator relies on what he can see to establish his position and to work out the direction to go. There is often little opportunity for regular chartwork. There are many landmarks: such as headlands, lighthouses, churches, water towers. There are also buoys and beacons. Using these as signposts to establish the boat's present position and where to go next is **pilotage**. Should the visibility deteriorate and the signposts disappear, then it will be necessary to start plotting on the chart; and pilotage becomes navigation.

Referring to chart 15, let us imagine that we are in a yacht entering Poole Harbour from a position 50° 39'.2N 1° 54'.8W close to the Poole Fairway buoy. It is a sunny day, the visibility is good, there is a light following breeze and there is a flood tide (so both the wind and tide are fair). The boat's speed is 4 knots. Looking to the north-west we can see the harbour entrance by the Haven Hotel in the distance and the Training Bank marked by beacons off to port. The chart shows the twin lines of green (starboard hand) and red (port hand) buoys leading towards the entrance (Plate 2). Keeping to the right of the channel (in accordance with the rules of the road) it is easy to sail from one green buoy to the next. Measure the distance from the Fairway buoy to the harbour entrance: it is about 2.3M (nautical miles). At 4 knots with a fair tidal stream we should reach the entrance in 30 minutes. We can then enter the harbour; but watch out for the chain ferry!

Lights and lighthouses

Lights used for navigational purposes are indicated with a magenta blob. They may be magnificent lighthouses or they may be sited in the windows of buildings. Often the light can be easily seen at night, but the light structure cannot be identified by day. Two lights in transit (leading lights)

Fig 9.1 The Conventional Direction of Buoyage in the British Isles follows the arrows shown

offer an ideal method of keeping within a channel (particularly if some
of the buoys are unlit). Sometimes a single light will have an intensified
sector on a certain bearing that marks the centre of a channel. Lights
may be sectored (White, Red, Green) to indicate potential hazards. The
end papers show a light (now discontinued) in position 50° 41'.1N 1°
56'.4W that marked the East Looe channel into Poole harbour. Under
East Looe channel in *Extract 6* (page 192) the characteristic is shown as
Oc WRG 6s 9m 10–6M and the sectors are given: Red 234°–294°; White
294°–304°; Green 304°–024°. By convention the bearings shown are true
directions as observed from *seaward*. The nominal range of the white
light is 10M, and of the red and green lights 6M.

Buoys and beacons

Buoys are plentiful in the approaches to commercial ports. For smaller
harbours and secondary channels beacons are used extensively.
Occasionally, down infrequently used channels, tree branches (called
withies) are stuck in the mud to indicate the deep water. When a vessel
is proceeding in the general direction of the buoyage or into harbour,
buoys marking the channel will be green conical shaped to starboard
and red can-shaped to port, Fig 9.1. Beacons will be green with conical
shaped topmarks to starboard and red with can shaped topmarks to port.
Figs 9.2 to 9.9 and Plates 2, 4, 5, 7, 10, 14, 21, 23, 25, 26 show buoys
and beacons used to mark channels and dangers.

For an unfamiliar passage, where a buoyed channel is to be followed,
it is a good idea to draw up a list of the buoys (or beacons) in the order
that they will be seen. Sufficient characteristics should be included so
that it will not be necessary to keep returning to the chart table. If there

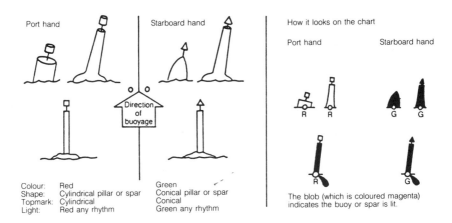

Colour:	Red	Green
Shape:	Cylindrical pillar or spar	Conical pillar or spar
Topmark:	Cylindrical	Conical
Light:	Red any rhythm	Green any rhythm

How it looks on the chart

The blob (which is coloured magenta) indicates the buoy or spar is lit.

Fig. 9.2 Lateral marks

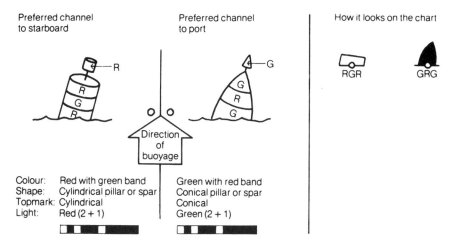

Fig 9.3 Preferred channel marks

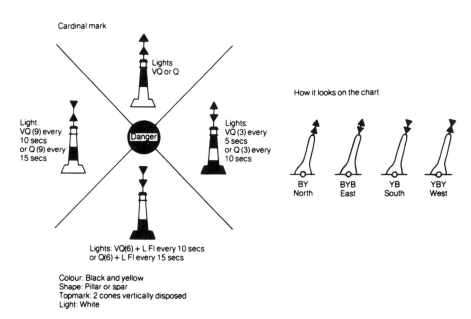

These marks are positioned to the north, east, south or west of danger.

Fig 9.4 Cardinal marks

How it looks on the chart

BRB

Colour: Red and black horizontal bands
Shape: Pillar or spar
Topmark: 2 spheres vertically disposed
Light: White, group flashing (2)

Fig 9.5 Isolated danger

How it looks on the chart

RW   RW   RW

Colour: Red and white vertical stripes
Shape: Spherical pillar or spar
Topmark: Red sphere
Light: White-isophase, occulting or morse letter A

This mark indicates that there is safe water around it.

Fig 9.6 Safe water mark

How it looks on the chart

Y   Y   Y

Colour: Yellow
Shape: Optional
Topmark: Cross
Light: Yellow

These are not navigational marks but have a special meaning which may be indicated on the chart. The shape is optional but must not conflict with navigational marks in the area.

This mark is over an isolated danger where there is navigable water all around it.

Fig 9.7 Special mark

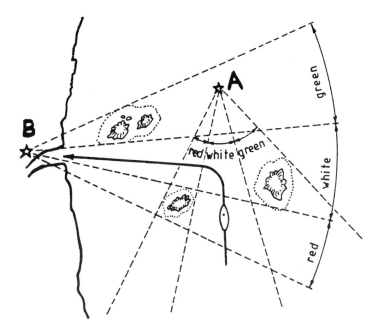

Fig 9.8 Sectored lights. Many lights have sectors of different colour: here the vessel must keep in the white sector of light A until she reaches the white sector of light B, when she can turn to port

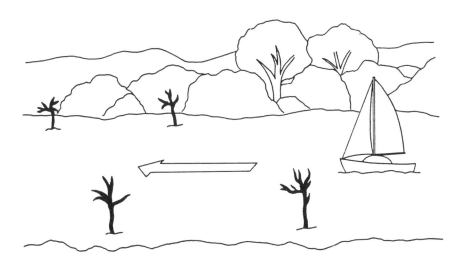

Fig 9.9 Withies. Further up the river: tree branches may be stuck in the mud to mark the edge of the channel

is any doubt about visibility, the direction and distance of the next mark (buoy or beacon) should be noted, Fig 9.10.

At night particular attention needs to be paid to the light characteristics of those buoys and beacons that are lit, Fig 9.11. From low down in a boat it is very difficult to judge distances, so the lights must be ticked

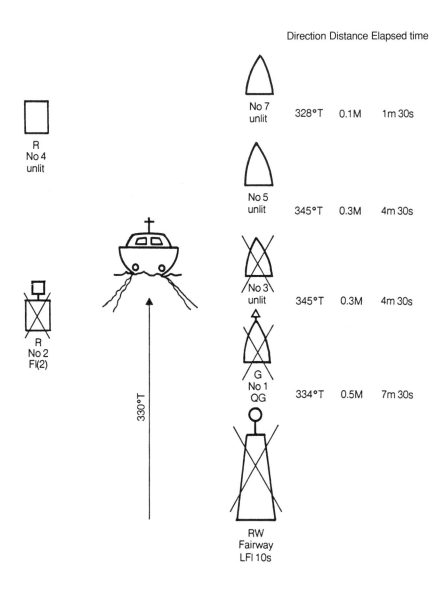

Fig 9.10 A buoyage plan

off (on our list) as they are passed. A watch with a second hand (or a digital stop watch) is useful for checking the characteristics of lights. Remember, too, that lights on buoys are not often visible at distances greater than two nautical miles. If the colour of a light is not indicated it is assumed to be white.

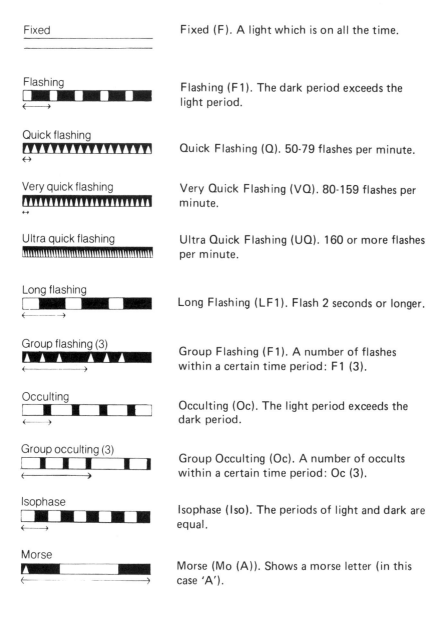

Fixed

Fixed (F). A light which is on all the time.

Flashing

Flashing (Fl). The dark period exceeds the light period.

Quick flashing

Quick Flashing (Q). 50-79 flashes per minute.

Very quick flashing

Very Quick Flashing (VQ). 80-159 flashes per minute.

Ultra quick flashing

Ultra Quick Flashing (UQ). 160 or more flashes per minute.

Long flashing

Long Flashing (LFl). Flash 2 seconds or longer.

Group flashing (3)

Group Flashing (Fl). A number of flashes within a certain time period: Fl (3).

Occulting

Occulting (Oc). The light period exceeds the dark period.

Group occulting (3)

Group Occulting (Oc). A number of occults within a certain time period: Oc (3).

Isophase

Isophase (Iso). The periods of light and dark are equal.

Morse

Morse (Mo (A)). Shows a morse letter (in this case 'A').

Fig 9.11 Light characteristics

Leading lines

One of the most helpful guides to entering or leaving an unfamiliar harbour are leading lines. They consist of two readily identifiable marks (or lights at night) which, when kept in line or in transit, indicate the direction of the safe water channel or harbour entrance, Plate 3. Make a note from the chart of the direction (or bearing) of the transit line: sometimes it is difficult to identify one of the transit marks or lights and knowing where to look relative to the other is important.

Transits

To keep two objects in line or in transit does not require them to be designated as a leading line. Any two objects identifiable on a chart can be used to indicate a desired direction or bearing, Plate 17. In open water a good way to compensate for a crossing tidal stream (a cross tide) is to keep the destination, which may well be a buoy, in transit with any fixed point on the coastline. The use of a transit on the approach to an anchorage is recommended, Fig 9.12.

Clearing bearings

Underwater hazards or dangers are not always marked by buoys or beacons. In the approaches to a harbour there is usually an identifiable

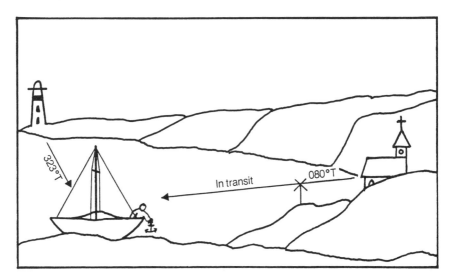

Fig 9.12 Boat anchors when the beacon and the church are in transit and the lighthouse bears 323°T

landmark in the locality. From the chart a line from this landmark passing clear of the hazard is determined. The direction of this line, represented as a bearing of the landmark, is known as a **clearing bearing**. From safe water if this bearing is not crossed, then the boat will not be in danger from the hazard, Fig 9.13.

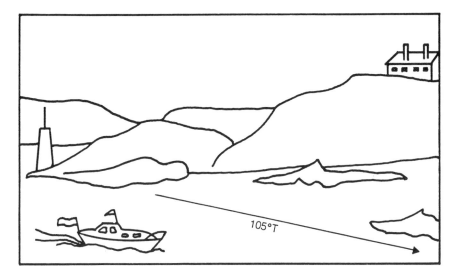

Fig 9.13 A clearing bearing. Provided the beacon bears more than 105°T the boat is in safe water

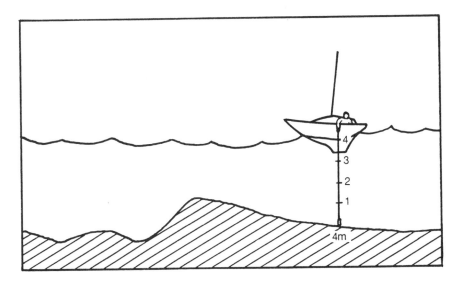

Fig 9.14 The depth of water can be found by using a lead marked in metres

Depth contours

The depth of water in the boat's present position is measured using an instrument known as a depth-sounder or echo-sounder, or by using a lead line (a heavy weight on the end of a line knotted at one metre intervals), Fig 9.14.

A line joining points on the seabed of equal depth is known as a **depth contour**. In areas where these contours are fairly straight they can be used either as a position line or as an indication of the edge of a channel, Fig 9.15.

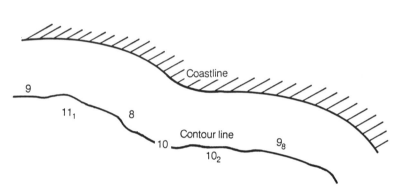

Fig 9.15 A depth contour

Nautical publications

These should be used with an up-to-date chart for pilotage and passage planning.

1. Tide tables.
2. Tidal stream atlas.
3. List of radio signals.
4. List of lights and fog signals.
5. Sailing directions or pilots.

These are available as separate hydrographic publications which are corrected by reference to Admiralty Notices to Mariners, by supplements or by re-issue. Also available from commercial firms is a yachtsman's almanac containing all the above information. *The Macmillan and Silk Cut Almanac* is an example. There are many commercial pilotage books suitable for the small craft user such as Adlard Coles *Pilot Packs* and *Normandy and Channel Islands Pilot* published by Adlard Coles Nautical, and the *Cruising Association Handbook*. Large scale Stanfords charts include pilotage information on the reverse side.

QUESTIONS

Use Extract 6

9.1a.   Describe Anvil Point light:
      i. by day   ii. by night
  b.   Approaching the light at night, at what distance, approximately, would it first be seen? (Assume a height of eye of 2m and that it is high water.)
  c.   How would you recognise the lighthouse in fog?

9.2   In a position 50° 37′.2N 1° 54′.7W, is it possible to use Anvil Point lighthouse for a bearing? What other landmarks are suitable for a bearing?

9.3   A boat is in estimated position 50° 40′.2N 1° 55′.0W. The original plan had been to locate East Hook buoy and then enter Poole harbour via the inshore passage; but there was a delay due to a fouled anchor and it is now dark. The navigator sights a quick flashing red light on a bearing of 320°M and a white light showing a long flash every 10 seconds in transit with a flashing yellow light on a bearing of 184°M. Assuming that the tide is approaching high water, should he enter Poole harbour via the inshore passage; and, if so, describe the sequence of the passage as far as the main channel.

9.4   When approaching Poole entrance, a boat sees the chain ferry hoist a black ball on its seaward side. What does this indicate; and what action should a boat take?

9.5a.   A boat is in an estimated position 50° 35′.5N 1° 57′.0W is making for the anchorage off Swanage. The tidal stream is north-going. It is dark but the visibility is good. How can she keep clear of Peveril Ledge?
  b.   How can she identify Swanage pier by night?

Chapter Ten

Where Have We Been?

Estimated position

We have until now been using the chart for pilotage where we have known our position in relation to the navigational marks. However we will not always be in sight of such marks so, to keep a record of our progress, we estimate our position by recording the boat's course and distance

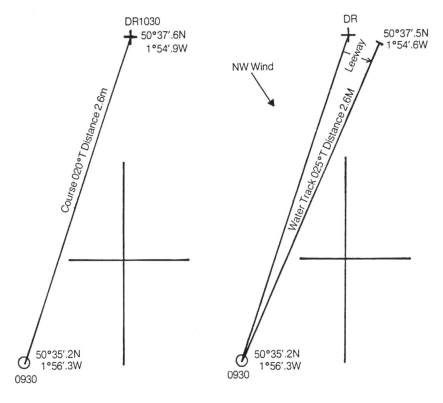

Fig 10.1 Dead reckoning   **Fig 10.2** Leeway

run together with estimated tidal streams and leeway (the sideways movement caused by the wind).

Let us assume that it is 0930 and we are in a position 50° 35'.2N 1° 56'.3W. From this position we steer a course of 020°T for a distance of 2.6M over a period of one hour. With no allowance for tidal stream or leeway, our 1030 position would be 50° 37'.6N 1° 54'.9W. This is a **dead reckoning (DR)** position, Fig 10.1, and is shown on the chart by using the symbol + .

(*Note:* Normally distances and speeds are rounded up to the nearest tenth of a mile or tenth of a knot. The large scale of chart 15 sometimes makes this difficult.)

However, a north west wind has pushed the boat off course through an angle of 5° so that the track of the boat through the water is 025°T. This sideways displacement is known as **leeway**. The track of the boat through the water is known as **water track**. Allowing for this leeway, the 1030 position is 50° 37'.5N 1° 54'.6W. In practice it is the water track which is plotted on the chart, not the true course, Fig 10.2.

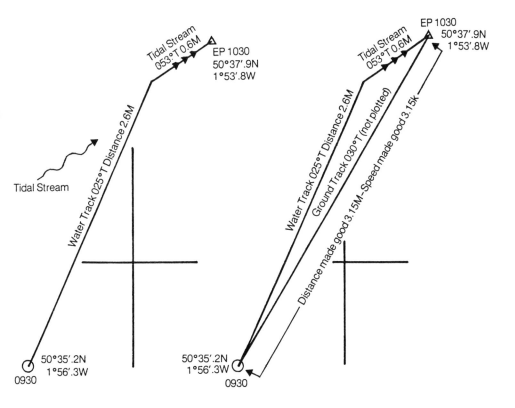

Fig 10.3 Tidal stream and estimated position

Fig 10.4 Ground track distance and speed made good

There is also a tidal stream setting towards the direction 053°T at a rate of 0.6 knots. A **knot** is the equivalent of one nautical mile per hour, and is usually indicated by the suffix 'k' or 'kn'. We must allow for this tidal stream. We plot it from the end of the water track, Fig 10.3.

The resultant position at 1030 now takes into account both leeway and tidal stream. It is known as an **estimated position (EP)** and is marked on the chart with the symbol △ . The EP is 50° 37'.9N 1° 53'.8W.

In the example the boat's speed was 2.6k (2.6M in one hour). The line drawn from the 0930 fix to the 1030 EP is known as the **ground track** and represents the effective track of the boat over the land (as opposed to through the water), Fig 10.4. The distance along the ground track from the 0930 fix to the 1030 EP is the **distance made good over the ground** or just **distance made good (DMG)**. In this example the distance made good is 3.15M (rounded to 3.2M). The **speed made good (SMG)** is the distance made good over a period of one hour; which, in this example, is 3.15 (3.2)k. Do not confuse the boat's speed through the water (2.6k) with her speed made good over the ground (3.2k). (*Note:* The ground track is not normally plotted.)

Estimated positions are usually plotted at hourly intervals; but may be plotted for any period of time. In the above example let us find the EP at 1000; which represents a time period of 30 minutes. The water track is still 025° but the distance run is 1.3M (which is the distance travelled at a speed of 2.6k for 30 minutes). The tidal stream is still 053° but the **drift** (distance that the water moves relative to the ground) is 0.3M (0.6k for 30 minutes). We now have the 1000 estimated position and can measure the distance made good between 0930 and 1000 which is 1.6M, Fig 10.5. Note that the speed made good is equivalent to the distance made good divided by the time (in hours): in this example it is still 3.2k.

The triangle formed by the water track, the tidal stream and the ground track is known as a **vector triangle**.

For a passage of several hours the estimated position can be derived by plotting the DR position for the passage then including all the tidal streams consecutively, Fig 10.6. Note that the resultant ground track only represents the mean of the course and tidal streams over the *duration* of the passage.

Time to tack

If a sailing boat is beating to windward, she may wish to know the time at which to tack in order to reach her destination. Firstly determine the best course that the helmsman can steer on each tack and then convert these two courses to water tracks. The better tack with which to start is that which keeps the boat's ground track nearest to the direct course

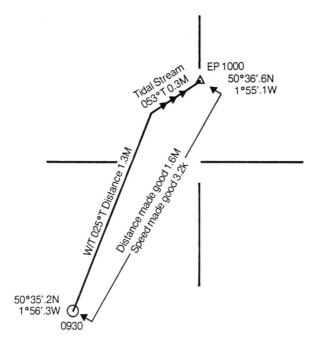

Fig 10.5 A half-hour vector

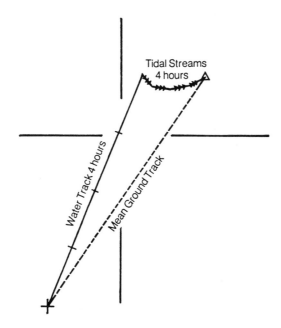

Fig 10.6 Estimated position after 4 hours

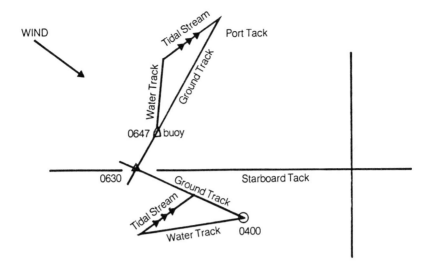

Fig 10.7 Time to tack

to the destination. From the starting point draw on the chart the ground track for the next hour (or half hour if the distance to go is small), Fig 10.7. Estimate roughly the time to tack and the approximate duration of the passage on the second tack. For the period of this duration (rounded to the nearest hour or half hour) draw on the chart *from the destination* the ground track for the second tack. (Note that this is only a construction so it does not matter where the lines go.) Project backwards this ground track to intersect the ground tack of the first tack. The point of intersection of the two ground tracks is the position of the change of track. Measure the distance and speed made good along each track and work out the **time to tack** and the **ETA** (estimated time of arrival) at the destination.

QUESTIONS

Use chart 15 and variation 5°W

10.1 At 1215, log 22.4, a motor boat steering a course of 019°M is in a position 50° 35'.5N 1° 54'.5W. The tidal stream is 053°T 0.8k. At 1245 the log reads 24.3M.

  a. Plot the DR position at 1245.
  b. Plot the EP at 1245.
  c. What is the direction of the ground track?
  d. What is the speed made good?

10.2   At 0430 a boat sailing at 5k on a course of 355°M is in position 50° 36'.7N 1° 48'.6W. At 0500 she tacks on to a course of 095°M. Leeway is negligible. The tidal stream is 057°T 1.0k. Plot the EP at 0530.

10.3   At 0830, log 20.9, a boat fixes her position as 086°T from Swanage pierhead 1.5M. She steers a course of 006°M. At 0900, log 22.6, she arrives at Poole Fairway buoy. What has been the direction and rate of the tidal stream between 0830 and 0900?

10.4   At 1150 a boat, sailing a course of 051°M at a speed of 4.0k, is in a position 50° 35'.5N 1° 55'.5W. Leeway is 10° due to a north wind. At 1250 she tacks to a course of 320°M. HW Portsmouth is at 1720 BST; it is neaps. Plot the EPs at 1250 and 1320. Use tidal diamond A for the first hour and tidal diamond B thereafter.

10.5   The following is an extract from the log of a boat on passage from Christchurch to Poole:

Time		Log	Course	Dev	Wind	Leeway
1600	Position 159°T CG Lookout 0.5M Sounding 12.8m	1.3	286°C	3°W	N6	5°
1700	Bournemouth pierhead bears 297°M Altered course to 233°C	5.4	233°C	2°W	N5	Nil
1703	Yellow buoy close abeam to starboard	5.6	233°C	2°W	N5	Nil
1749	Red buoy 0.2M on port beam. Engine started. Altered course to 312°C	8.3	312°C	4°W	N5	Nil

Tidal stream between 1600 and 1700: 275°T 0.2k
Tidal stream between 1700 and 1800: Negligible

Plot the EPs at 1700 and 1749. Identify the red buoy abeam at 1749.

Chapter Eleven

Finding Our Position

Position lines

In the last chapter we found out how to estimate our position in the absence of suitable navigational marks. Whereas it is essential to keep a record throughout a passage of the estimated position, accurate positions should be plotted where possible using bearings of suitable land and sea marks which can be identified both visually and on the chart.

We normally use the hand-bearing compass to take the bearings to fix our position. Referring to the south west corner of chart 15 and assuming we are in a DR position (approximate) of 50° 35'.2N 1° 55'.4W, we take these bearings:

Anvil Point lighthouse	298°M
Durlston Head	320°M
Peveril Point	357°M

We will plot these bearings using the protractor scale on the parallel rule. First we convert the magnetic bearings to true bearings allowing for the local variation which is 4°W:

Anvil Point lighthouse	294°T
Durlston Head	316°T
Peveril Point	353°T

Place the rule across the meridian nearest to Anvil Point lighthouse so that it passes through the south point of the protractor scale at the bearing of 294°. Both edges of the rule now lie along the direction of the bearing (and its reciprocal). It may be possible to line up the rule so that an edge also passes through Anvil Point lighthouse, but, if not, we will need to walk the rule so that an edge passes through the lighthouse. Draw a line from the lighthouse in the opposite direction to the bearing: this line is called a **position line** and will have an arrowhead on the end furthest from the lighthouse. In practice only that part of the position line in the vicinity of the DR position is drawn. We know that our position is somewhere along this position line. A second position line which crosses the first will give our exact position at the point of intersection. To verify the accuracy a third position line (from a bearing taken at the same time) should pass through the same point.

But looking at Fig 11.1 the three position lines do not intersect at a common point but form a triangle (known as a **cocked hat**). The variation has been correctly applied. The error is due to incorrect identification of Durlston Head because of its 'end on' aspect. There is a prominent castle on Durlston Head which makes a better landmark. The bearing of the castle is 319°M or 315°T which gives a much better fix, Fig 11.2.

In practice if three bearings are taken to give three position lines, it is quite likely that a small cocked hat will result particularly if the boat is moving fast or if there is a rough sea. Provided there are no immediate hazards the centre of a small cocked hat is acceptable as the boat's position. If there is a hazard on the course ahead, assume a position at the corner of the cocked hat nearest the hazard. A large cocked hat may be caused by applying the variation in the wrong sense; but if that is not the case the bearings should be taken again. Ideally two position lines should cross at right angles and three position lines should have a relative difference of 60°. Avoid the temptation to take bearings of objects at greater distances particularly if there are others nearby. Buoys can be out of position so land based objects are preferred. A position obtained from two or more bearings of landmarks (or buoys) is known

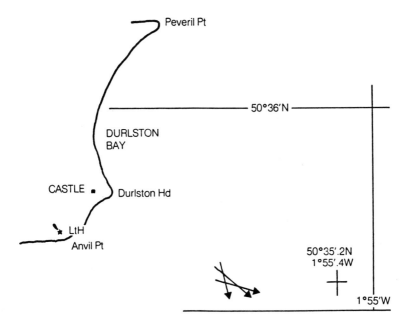

Fig 11.1 A cocked hat

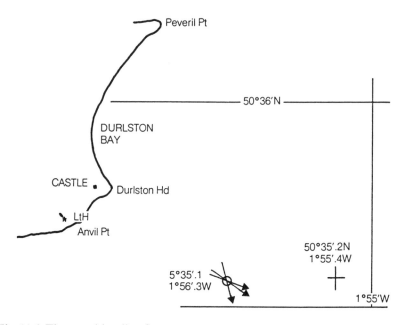

Fig 11.2 Three position line fix

as a **fix** and is indicated on a chart using the symbol $\odot$. Any position on a chart *must* have the time marked beside it; and it is also desirable to make a note of the log reading (in the form of distance travelled).

Other considerations when taking bearings are:

1. Nearer objects are preferred to distant ones as angular differences will cause smaller errors.
2. Bearings ahead and astern should be taken first as bearings abeam alter more rapidly.
3. The use of left or right hand edges of headlands is acceptable provided they are steep.
4. Off-lying features may merge with the background and be difficult to locate.
5. Spot heights are useful for identifying sections of a coastline but they are no good for bearings as the highest point on the chart may not in fact be visible from the boat.
6. At night lights must be positively identified from their characteristics. Car headlights or fishing boats bobbing up and down on the waves sometimes give the appearance of the lights of a lighthouse or a buoy.

Transferred position line or running fix

If at any moment we obtain a bearing of a single landmark and sometime later we obtain another single bearing, provided these bearings are different by around 90° we can determine our position.

For example, refer to Fig 11.3. At 1145 Peveril Point bears 352°T. The boat continues on a course of 020°T at a speed of 2.6k with a north west wind causing 5° of leeway. The tidal stream is 053°T 0.6k. At 1215 Peveril Point bears 265°T.

The 1145 position line is plotted on the chart. From *any* point on this line (but normally the closest point to the 1145 DR position) the water track (025°T) is plotted for the distance travelled between 1145 and 1215 (1.3M). For the same time period the tidal stream (053°T 0.3M) is added. The point obtained is an EP relative to the starting point on the 1145 position line. The second position line taken at 1215 is plotted. The first position line is now transferred to pass through the EP and to cross the second position line. The point of intersection is the 1215 position. This method of obtaining a fix is known as a **running fix** or a **transferred**

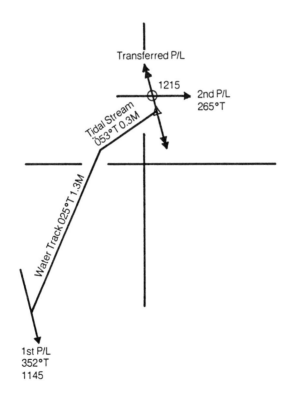

Fig 11.3 Transferred position line

position line. The accuracy of a running fix depends on the assessment of the boat's course and speed, the leeway, and the tidal stream. It is not as good a fix as one obtained from two or more bearings taken at the same time.

Radiobeacons

A marine radiobeacon is marked on the chart with the (magenta) symbol: (⊙)^RC An aeronautical radiobeacon is marked on the chart with the symbol: (⊙)^Aero RC

A **radio direction finder** or **RDF** is used to identify and obtain a bearing of a radiobeacon provided it is within range. This bearing can then be used as a position line for a fix.

Yachtsman's almanacs contain a list of radiobeacons showing their position, frequency, identity signal, transmission time and range. Marine radiobeacons normally transmit within a period of a minute the identity signal (repeated several times), a continuous tone, and then the identity signal again. With the radio direction finder tuned to the correct frequency, the radiobeacon is first identified, then the antenna is rotated in the horizontal plane during the period of continuous tone until the signal level drops to a minimum (known as a 'null'). From the magnetic compass on the antenna the bearing is read at the instant of the null. Whilst the bearings of radiobeacons are being taken, the helmsman must be encouraged to steer a steady course.

There is a null both when the antenna is directly towards the radiobeacon and when it is pointing directly away. It is usually quite evident which is correct if the radiobeacon is on the coastline. For a radiobeacon on an island or lightship, set a course temporarily at right angles to the bearing of the radiobeacon: if the bearing increases the radiobeacon is on the starboard side; if it decreases, the radiobeacon is to port.

An aeronautical radiobeacon transmits the continuous tone with the identity signals superimposed and without any breaks.

The radio beam is refracted (bent) when it passes either from land to sea or at a narrow angle to the coast so any bearings obtained may be unreliable. Radio distortion frequently occurs at the time of dusk and dawn. It is not easy without practice to obtain a good bearing of a radiobeacon.

Line of soundings

An echo-sounder is an instrument used to measure the depth of water. (The depth measured is actually between the seabed and the sensor or transducer mounted on the boat's hull.) The depth of water when

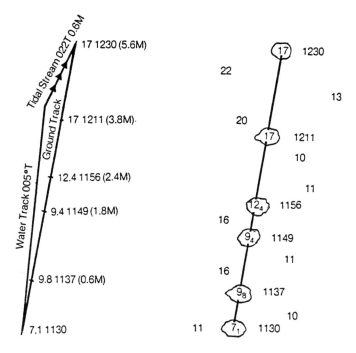

Fig 11.4 Running a line of soundings

corrected for the height of tide corresponds with the depths shown on the chart (called **soundings**). If a boat crossing a shelving seabed records corrected depths at regular time intervals or regular distances from the log readings, a **line of soundings** is obtained, Fig 11.4.

This line of soundings is marked on a strip of paper which can be placed alongside the ground track on the chart and moved forwards or backwards to obtain a correlation with the depths shown on the chart.

If the depth contours (usually 5m, 10m, 15m) on the chart are regular (fairly straight lines), they can be used as underwater position lines. By following a depth contour (altering course to remain in a constant depth of water) it is frequently possible to skirt round an underwater hazard in conditions of poor visibility (see Depth contours: Chapter 9).

Comparison of methods to determine position

1. Two or more visual bearings: very accurate provided that there is a good angle of cut between the position lines.
2. Two or more radio bearings: difficult except where suitable radiobeacons are available.

3. Transferred position line: only as accurate as the assessment of water track, distance run and tidal stream.
4. Line of soundings: the approximate position of the boat must be known and there must be distinguishable features on the seabed.
5. Estimated position: the best estimate of the boat's position, taking into account the accuracies of the course steered, the distance run, the leeway and the direction and rate of the tidal stream.
   Dead reckoning: the position obtained *only* from the course steered and distance run.

(*Note:* Close inshore, there may not be time to fix the boat's position. A leading line allows a rapid appreciation of any tendency for the boat to be set off track. Clearing bearings help ensure that navigational hazards are avoided. An echo-sounder should always be used for verification of position.)

QUESTIONS

Use chart 15 and variation 5°W

11.1 At 1400 a motor boat in an estimated position 50° 35′.4N 1° 57′.2W takes the following bearings using the hand-bearing compass:

> Anvil Point lighthouse   345°M
> Castle on Durlston Head   040°M

a. Plot fix.

b. As only two bearings were available, what could be done to check the accuracy of the fix?

c. Assuming the log is accurate, what may account for the difference between the EP and the fix?

11.2 The same boat continues on a course of 263°C. At 1420 she sights two beacons in transit. The bearing of these beacons on the steering compass is 355°C and on the hand-bearing compass 359°M.

a. What is the deviation of the steering compass?

b. Can this deviation be used for any heading of the boat?

c. Is there any deviation on the hand-bearing compass?

d. Can the hand-bearing compass be assumed to have any deviation?

11.3 At 1130, log 3.8, a boat, steering a course of 014°M, is in a DR position 50°35′.2N 1° 55′.4W. She takes a bearing of Anvil Point lighthouse: 284°M.

At 1200, log 5.7, the right-hand edge of Handfast Point bears 353°M. The west wind is causing 5° of leeway. The tidal stream between 1130 and 1230 is 049°T 1.0k.

a. Plot the position at 1200.

b. What is the accuracy of the 1200 position?

c. How would you write this position as a direction and distance from Handfast Point?

11.4   At 0930 a boat in DR position 50° 42'.5N 1° 51'.0W takes the following bearings using a hand-bearing compass:

Bournemouth Pier	286°M
Boscombe Pier	052°M
Conspicuous hotel in Bournemouth (right hand edge)	005°M
Yellow buoy (off Bournemouth Pier)	267°M

a. Plot fix.

b. What comments can you make about the bearings?

11.5   At 0915 on a course of 094°M a boat takes a bearing of the CG Lookout on Hengistbury Head: 050°M. At the same time the echo-sounder reads 11.0m. The height of tide is estimated as 0.8m. The boat's draught is 2.0m and the transducer of the echo-sounder is 0.3m below the waterline.

a. Is this a positive fix?

b. Should the boat take any action?

Chapter Twelve

How To Get There

Course to steer

We need to know our present position both to be sure that we are clear of any hazards and to determine the direction and distance to the next point on our way or passage (a **waypoint**). On a large scale chart (such as chart 15) we can draw in the desired ground track from waypoint to waypoint and then check our position at regular intervals to ensure that we are close enough to the track and clear of any potential dangers. For longer passages and in poor visibility we must be able to work out the course to steer to the next waypoint compensating for the tidal stream, leeway, variation and deviation with the same degree of accuracy that we required for working out our estimated position (see Chapter 10).

Referring to chart 15, let us assume that at 0900 we are in position 50° 35'.9N 1° 52'.5W and we want to know the course to steer to Poole Fairway buoy in position 50° 39'.0N 1° 54'.8W. We first draw a line from our 0900 position to the buoy. This line represents our desired ground track, Fig 12.1.

The distance along the ground track is 3.4M. If we were able to sail directly along the ground track with no leeway or tidal stream, at a speed of 4k we would reach the buoy in 51 minutes at 0951.

$$\frac{3.4}{4} \times 60 = 51 \text{ minutes: that is } 0951.$$

If there was a tidal stream setting towards 046°T at 1.3k we make allowances in the following manner. The time to reach the buoy will be (as an initial rough estimate) about one hour, so we will use one hour's worth of tidal stream: 046°T 1.3M. The tidal stream is drawn *from the 0900 position*, Fig 12.2.

In one hour the boat will have travelled through the water a distance of 4.0M. Using the dividers measure a distance of 4.0M on the latitude scale. With one point of the dividers on the end of the tidal stream vector, place the other point of the dividers on the ground track (extending the ground track if necessary) and mark this position. The line from the end of the tidal stream vector to this position is the water track. The

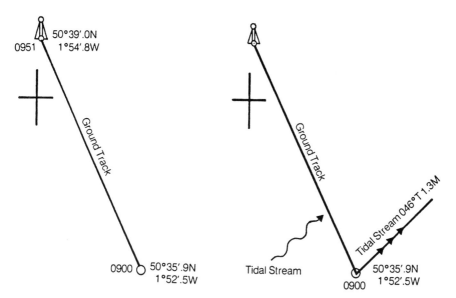

Fig 12.1 Ground track

Fig 12.2 Tidal stream

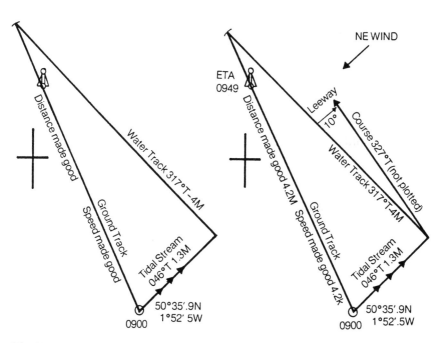

Fig 12.3 Water track distance
and speed made good

Fig 12.4 Leeway and true course

position marked will be the estimated position *after one hour*, that is at 1000, Fig 12.3. We now measure the direction of the water track: 317°T.

In order that the water track can be converted to the correct course to steer to achieve the desired ground track, we have to compensate for any leeway by steering into the wind: *towards* the direction from which the wind is blowing. If there was a wind from the north east causing 10° of leeway, we would need to steer a course of 327°T, Fig 12.4.

The **course to steer** is the course given to the helmsman, so it must include corrections for compass variation and (if necessary) deviation. With a variation of 5°W and zero deviation, our course to steer is 332°C.

The speed made good is the distance made good for a period of one hour as measured along the ground track between the positions at 0900 and 1000. It is 4.2k (Fig 12.4).

We may need to know our **Estimated Time of Arrival** or **ETA** at the buoy. The 1000 estimated position is beyond the buoy so we will take less than one hour to reach the buoy. From the 0900 position the

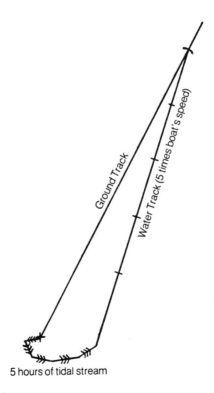

5 hours of tidal stream

Fig 12.5 Plotting 5-hour vector

distance to the buoy, measured along the ground track, is 3.4M. The speed made good is 4.2k. The time taken to reach the buoy is 49 minutes.

$$\frac{3.4}{4.2} \times 60 = 49 \text{ minutes.}$$

So the ETA at the Poole Fairway buoy is 0949.

There is no need to use a period of one hour. For instance on a large scale chart a half-hour period may be more suitable. The distances drawn would correspond to half an hour of tidal stream and half an hour of boat speed giving the distance made good in half an hour (so speed made good would be twice the distance made good). For a long passage of 5 hours the tidal streams over that period are aggregated together from the starting point; a distance of 5 times the boat's speed is drawn from the tidal stream vectors to the ground track, this line being the water track and the point of intersection with the ground track being the estimated position for a time 5 hours after the start, Fig 12.5. In this

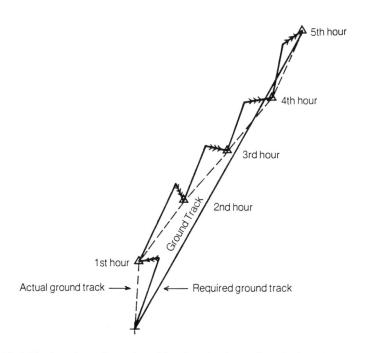

Fig 12.6 Plotting the estimated position hourly shows that the boat is near the required ground track but not on it until the fifth hour

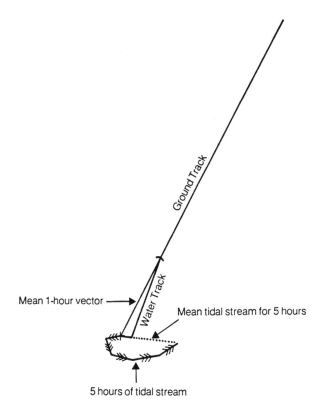

Fig 12.7 Plotting a one-hour vector using the mean tidal stream for 5 hours

case, whilst we can make a reasonable estimate of the course to steer (from the water track), the boat may well not be on the ground track until the end of the passage, Fig 12.6. An alternative is to determine the mean tidal stream over a period of time and apply it on an hourly basis, Fig 12.7.

QUESTIONS

Use chart 15 and variation 5°W

12.1 A boat at Poole Fairway buoy wishes to make good a ground track of 060°T. Her speed is 4.0k. The tidal stream is 344°T 0.7k. Wind SE. Leeway 10°. What is the magnetic course to steer?

12.2 A boat at Boscombe Pier at 1750 BST is heading towards Poole Fairway buoy at a speed of 4.0k. What is the magnetic course to steer? What is her ETA? Use tidal diamond B; HW Portsmouth 1420, springs Wind NW5, leeway, 5°.

12.3   At 1550 a boat is in a position 50° 37'.0N 1° 49'.5W. What is the magnetic course to steer at a speed of 2.5k to Poole Fairway buoy? Use tidal diamond A for the first hour and tidal diamond B for the remainder. Wind S, leeway 10°. HW Portsmouth 1923, neaps. What is the ETA at the buoy?

12.4   At 1150 a boat is in a position 50° 35'.4N 1° 55'.5W. Wind N, leeway 10°. At a speed of 3k, she needs to make good a ground track of 050°T. Use tidal diamond A for first hour; then tidal diamond B. HW Portsmouth 1720; neaps. She tacks at 1250. What is the magnetic course to Poole Fairway buoy and what is the ETA?

12.5   At 0900 BST a motor boat is in a position 095°T Anvil Point lighthouse 1.5M. What is the magnetic course to steer to the position 084°T Old Harry rock 1.0M? Leeway nil. Speed 6k. HW Portsmouth 1515; springs. Use tidal diamond B.

Chapter Thirteen

What Part Does the Weather Play?

Mist and fog

One of the worst hazards at sea is poor visibility. All visual landmarks disappear. Consequently electronic aids to navigation become more desirable and should be constantly monitored. It is also essential to plot the DR or EP regularly. If fog is forecast, frequent fixes must be taken until landmarks are no longer visible. A steady course should be steered and distance run measured with an instrument called a log, which must be accurate. Be prepared to change the passage destination for one which can be safely reached before visibility deteriorates. It is relatively straightforward to avoid underwater obstructions; the main problem is collision with other vessels. Always travel at a safe speed.

Visibility is defined as: *very good* – more than 30 miles; *good* – 5–30 miles; *moderate* – 2–5 miles; *poor* – less than 2 miles; *mist* or haze – 1000–2000 metres; *fog* – less than 1000 metres; *thick fog* – less than 366 metres.

However, suppose we set out on a clear sunny day not expecting any changes. The horizon has become indistinct; the fishing boat that we have passed is becoming blurred; the sun's rays seem less warming: definite signs of an approaching fog-bank. What actions should we take?

1. *Get a fix.* Try to get a fix of the boat's position by any means available. Record the time and log reading. If this is not possible, then work out the estimated position from the last known position. Draw on the chart the anticipated course and DR positions for the next few hours. Check the availability of radio navigation aids. Switch on the echo-sounder and navigation lights.
2. *Note positions and direction of travel of any other shipping*, particularly any vessels that might pass close by.
3. *Take safety precautions.* Hoist radar reflector; check fog signalling apparatus; don lifejackets; check that the liferaft is ready to launch;

inflate the dinghy and tow it astern; if under sail, check that the engine is ready to start immediately; post a look-out in the bows; maintain silence; brief all crew on deck to listen for fog signals from other vessels.

4 . *Review the passage plan.* Decide whether to maintain the present course and destination, go out to sea, or anchor in shallow water.

5 . If following a buoyed channel, *list the buoys and their characteristics, with distances and directions from one buoy to the next.* Tick each buoy as it is passed and compare elapsed time with distance run. Use an echo-sounder to keep within the channel and be aware upon which side of the boat the deeper water lies.

6 . *Approaching a harbour* clear of any outlying dangers, *set a course towards one side of the entrance.* When the shoreline is sighted or a particular depth contour reached, there is no doubt which way to alter course for the harbour entrance. With a strong tidal stream across the entrance, set a course well upstream so that the tidal stream will be fair when the shoreline is sighted.

7 . *Listen for the fog signals of lighthouses.* It is not easy to determine the direction of sound in fog. A radio direction finder can help to find a harbour entrance by keeping a lighthouse radio beacon on a constant bearing.

Strong winds

Slow-moving zones of high pressure give settled and stable weather. There can be strong winds but they are usually steady in strength and direction. Areas of low pressure cause unsettled weather with much cloud, poor visibility, rain, and winds which vary in strength and direction. In the northern hemisphere, air circulates in a clockwise direction in a high pressure system and an anti-clockwise direction in a low pressure system.

It is important to record barometric pressure, wind strength and direction regularly and to observe cloud formation.

For a small boat of length less than 9 metres a wind of strength (force) 6, which is a wind speed of 25 knots, is normally the limit of comfortable sailing. A larger boat may be able to cope with gale force 8 (35 knots). The Beaufort Wind Scale is shown in Extract 8 page 193.

Running downwind is more comfortable than beating to windward. However, it is the combination of wind and sea-state that affect the ability of a sailing boat to make a safe passage in strong winds. If the wind is blowing in the opposite direction to the tidal stream, the sea may become very rough particularly at spring tides. Under these conditions shallow water, tide races and overfalls can become dangerous even though the charted depth may be adequate. In open seas a wave pattern can build up which is not particularly hazardous in itself, but if the wind changes another wave pattern can be superimposed on the original which causes very rough seas. This effect can also occur near (within a half mile) of a sea wall where the reflected wave is superimposed on the original.

Provided a boat is well constructed and equipped, the sails are reefed, and the crew are not prone to seasickness, then strong winds need be no deterrent to the completion of a passage provided sensible precautions are observed. More prudence may be required before setting off on a long passage with a forecast of strong winds and the following precautions should be observed:

1. Most emergencies in rough weather are caused by the failure of the crew rather than the boat. Tiredness, cold and hunger increase the likelihood of seasickness. If an extended sea passage is anticipated, let any crew not required go below to rest. Wind chill cools quicker than most people realise, so extra warm clothes must be put on early before shivering starts. A substantial hot meal before a night passage and at breakfast time is desirable; and frequent light snacks and drinks should be encouraged. If necessary make a large box of sandwiches. Above all, seasickness tablets must be taken well in advance; not just as the motion starts to deteriorate.

2. In a small boat it is very difficult to navigate in rough weather. Often the deck log is not kept up to date: with no log readings and course alterations recorded, it is impossible to estimate a position. Usually it is not easy to remain at the chart table for prolonged periods without feeling queasy. The solution is careful preparation. The charts should be stowed accessibly in the order that they will be required. All tidal information should be extracted from the almanac and recorded in a 'navigator's notebook'. On the tidal stream atlas or diagram, fill in the time of high water and the hours before and after high water. For all harbours along the route of the passage key information should be noted: direction of tidal streams in the approach; conspicuous landmarks; characteristics of lights and buoys; details of clearing bearings and transits. Each chart should be marked up with the route including the compass course for each change of direction; together with highlighting of all hazards and conspicuous landmarks, clearing bearings, and change-over positions from one chart to the next.

3. Secure the boat for sea. In a rough sea everything that can move will move. Keeping accessible those items that may be required, lash down or secure everything else so that it cannot shift about. Check all hatches are secure. The anchor may be better lashed inboard rather than over the bow.

4. Reef the sails early; it is much easier to increase sail if the wind drops than to shorten sail if the wind increases. When the wind increases enough for sails to be reefed all the crew on deck and in the cockpit

should be wearing safety harnesses and clip them on to the safety lines or strong points. Do not use guardrails for securing safety harnesses: they are not strong enough to take the snatch load of a person falling overboard.

5 . If it is decided to anchor (or remain in an anchorage), more anchor cable is necessary in strong winds. In fair weather if the anchor cable is all chain, then the simple rule is 4 × *maximum depth of water*; if the cable is a short length (6m) of chain backed by a nylon warp, then let out 6 × *maximum depth of water*. In strong winds let out 8 × *maximum depth of water*; and, if possible, let go a second anchor.

Lee shore

For hundreds of years seafaring yarns have recounted the hazards of a lee shore. If there is a shoreline on the leeward side of the boat (as opposed to the windward side) it is called a **lee shore**. It is a shoreline on to which the wind is blowing. A powerless vessel will be blown by the wind on to a lee shore. If the seabed gradually shelves upwards to the shore, then in strong onshore winds the waves will build up into breakers which will crash down on the coastline. Any vessel caught up in these breakers has little chance of survival. Any harbour with its entrance or approach open to windward becomes extremely hazardous in strong winds. A small craft at sea should keep clear of a lee shore in heavy weather and should not contemplate entering such a harbour. Not a happy decision for the skipper of a small boat with nightfall approaching and with a tired, cold and seasick crew.

Weather forecasts

To avoid some of the problems of poor visibility and strong winds, careful attention should be paid to weather forecasts. The sources can be summarised as follows:

1. *Shipping forecasts.* These are broadcast on BBC Radio 4 (long wave) at 0048, 0555, 1355 and 1750. BBC Radio 4 has a wavelength of 1515 metres which is equivalent to a frequency of 198 kilohertz (198 kHz). The forecast lists any gale warnings in force, gives a general synopsis of the weather patterns affecting the UK Continental Shelf, forecasts the weather over the next 24 hours for the sea areas surrounding the United Kingdom and gives details of the weather reported at coastal weather stations. While much of the detail may not be relevant, it is a most useful forecast for a small sailor contemplating a coastal passage.

2. *Inshore waters forecast.* This is broadcast on BBC Radio 4 after the shipping forecast at 0048 and on BBC Radio 3 at 0655. It is a fore-cast of the weather expected around the UK coastline (within 12 miles

of the coast) for the next 24 hours. Winds along the coastline are normally not as strong as in the open sea; but occasionally in local areas funnelling can cause strong winds.

3 . *Local radio forecasts.* Local radio stations broadcast weather reports and forecasts some of which specifically cover the requirements of sailing enthusiasts. The information is up to date and specific for a locality. Frequently additional information such as times of local high tides, shipping movements, and navigational warnings are included. Land weather forecasts contain much useful supplementary information.

4 . *Newspapers and television.* The synoptic charts in newspapers and on television are particularly useful for observing long-term trends in weather patterns in anticipation of a weekend sail or a cruise lasting several days. The information in newspapers is not up to date.

5 . *Marinecall.* A telephone call-in service specially for yachtsmen. Forecasts are given for specific coastal areas and are updated every six hours.

6 . *Weather centres.* The London Weather Centre and other local weather centres can be contacted for information on the weather forecast for periods up to 5 days ahead. A personal visit is better than telephoning.

7 . *Coastguard.* The Coastguard broadcast weather information at regular intervals. They will repeat the local forecast if requested on the VHF radio telephone (channel 67). They also broadcast strong wind warnings (Force 6 and above).

8. *Coastal radio stations (British Telecom).* Daily at 0703 or 0733 and at 1903 or 1933 (Greenwich Mean Time). Coast Radio Stations rebroadcast the shipping forecast for the local area.

9 . *Local air stations.* All air stations have a duty forecaster. If he is not busy he can provide a very good up to date local forecast.

1 0 . *Gale warnings.* On BBC Radio 4 gale warnings received from the Meteorological Office are broadcast at the next programme break after receipt and on completion of the next news bulletin. Gale warnings are also broadcast by the Coastguard and local radio stations in addition to strong winds warnings. A strong wind is Force 6 and above.

11. *MetFAX Marine.* For yachtsmen with access to a fax machine, a weather map and a 48 hour forecast can be obtained. An index is available by fax on 0336 400401.

QUESTIONS

See back of chart 15 and Extract 8 where appropriate

13.1   A navigator is about to plan a passage. Where can he obtain:
   a. the details of present and expected weather including wind direction and strength, visibility and sea state?

   b. the position and movement of weather systems likely to affect the passage and details of any gale warnings?

13.2   The 0555 shipping forecast is missed. Where can gale warnings, general synopsis, sea area forecast and reports from coast stations for a passage from Yarmouth to Swanage be obtained?

13.3   A motor boat is leaving Poole harbour on the ebb tide. Conditions are calm, visibility poor and deteriorating. The only landmark in sight is the beacon at the end of the Training Bank which is close to starboard. From dead ahead comes the sound of engines and a prolonged blast on a siren. What action should be taken?

13.4   The wind has been blowing SW 6–7 for the past two days but has now veered to NW 5. The following types of boat propose to leave Poole harbour on the ebb tide at springs to round Anvil Point continuing their passage to westward. How would you expect each boat to react to weather and sea state?
   a. Motor boat, length 10m, shallow draught, cruising speed 8k.
   b. Deep fin-keeled sailing boat, length 12m, cruising speed 7k.
   c. Twin bilge-keeled sailing boat, length 9m, cruising speed 5k.

13.5   What do the following terms mean:
   a. **poor** visibility
   b. a depression moving **rapidly**
   c. a **near gale**
   d. a **moderate breeze**
   e. **later**

Chapter Fourteen

Planning Ahead

Before embarking on any sea passage, whether it is just a trip out of the harbour or a voyage across the English Channel, it is necessary to plan things out well beforehand.

Here are some of the things to do:

1. All charts to be used should be checked to see whether they need updating and the latest *Notices to Mariners* obtained to see that no corrections have been missed. A visit to the Harbour Master's office usually pays dividends as he will have details of any activities or changes within the harbour limits such as dredging or maintenance of navigational marks.
2. A small-scale chart is needed initially to plan the voyage. Larger scale charts will be required for coastal passages. The largest scale charts will be required for harbours or anchorages.
3. Read the relevant sailing directions.
4. Look over the sails; check standing and running rigging, safety equipment, wet weather gear, cooking facilities and engine. Check the batteries. Check the dinghy and outboard motor. Ensure that the crew are familiar with the location of safety equipment and emergency procedures.
5. Start a record of the general weather pattern.
6. Work out the starting time for the voyage, taking into consideration tides and daylight hours. Check the tides at the destination, bearing in mind the opening times of locks and basins. Measure the mileage, inspect the tidal streams and make a rough estimate of the time to complete the passage allowing for the boat's normal cruising speed. Check times of sunrise and sunset, see Extract 7, p. 193. Fill in the tidal stream atlas. Draw in the proposed track and check for any hazards on the way. If using an electronic position fixing system, mark in the waypoints. Highlight any conspicuous landmarks. For a night passage, list the characteristics together with the visibility range and bearing of all lights likely to be encountered (remembering

that buoys are not generally visible at a range greater than 2M).
Establish alternative destinations in case of unforeseen circumstances.

7. Before the passage, fill up with water and fuel and check that a spare
   gas bottle (for the cooker) is on board. Stow all gear below and secure
   all items on deck. Get the latest weather forecast. Ensure that a
   responsible person ashore knows both the details of your passage
   and who will be on board. As soon as departure time is confirmed,
   work out the DR positions (and estimated positions if time) for the
   first leg of the passage.

8. As the harbour entrance is cleared, set the log to zero and give the
   helmsman the course to steer (assuming if under sail that the course
   to steer is not into the wind). As soon as the boat's speed can be
   established, check the estimated positions for the first part of the
   passage.

9. If the course to steer is into the wind, it is important to establish
   from the helmsman the best course he can steer on each tack. When
   beating to windward (making a series of tacks into the wind) the
   navigator will need to decide when to tack to make best use of any
   tidal streams and to keep clear of any navigational hazards. In
   anticipation of any shift in wind direction, keep within 5M of the
   desired track reducing this distance progressively as the destination
   or waypoint is approached. (Keep within a cone of 20° from the
   desired track as measured from the destination.)

10. Fix the boat's position regularly: at least every 30 minutes if within
    sight of land. Compare the estimated positions and fixes to make
    allowance for any deviation from the desired track. Record the log
    reading every hour; and the barometric pressure and wind direction
    and speed at least every four hours. The deck log should contain
    sufficient navigational information so that the broad details of the
    passage could be re-created at a later date.

11. If the weather conditions are deteriorating, be prepared to make
    for an alternative destination or to turn back.

12. When the ETA (estimated time of arrival) at the destination is
    established, re-check any restrictions due to tidal stream or height
    of tide. Be prepared to anchor or pick up a mooring near the
    entrance. Check for local signals restricting entry to the harbour
    or any tidal basins.

13. Frequently when entering an unfamiliar harbour it is not clear where
    a visitor should go initially. Use of a VHF radio (if available) to
    call up the local marina or harbour master is ideal. If visitor's
    moorings or berths can be identified, they should be used. Otherwise
    it may be necessary to secure to a vacant buoy or pontoon whilst
    seeking advice on berthing. Should the owner return meanwhile,
    at least he will be able to give guidance on an alternative berth;
    but be prepared to move at short notice.

Chapter Fifteen

An Extra Crew Member

A position finding system, such as Decca, Loran or a Satellite Navigator, is a valuable aid to navigation. Provided it is working satisfactorily it can give a constant read-out of the boat's present position. Normally the present position is based on a fix from two or three position lines obtained from bearings of landmarks taken with the hand-bearing compass. An electronic system does not require a landmark to be visible.

In all position finding systems the first objective is to establish the boat's position as a latitude and longitude. Additional selected positions, known as waypoints, can be entered and the computer will derive direction and distance from the boat's position to any of these waypoints or between any of the waypoints. Course and speed made good can also be displayed. Man overboard position markers are sometimes included. Some systems will work out tidal stream or current if the boat's course and speed are entered.

In conditions where navigation is difficult, such electronic aids make a significant contribution to safety. If a position fixing system is installed it should be used; but only to supplement the other methods of establishing a boat's position.

Radio and electronic aids

HYPERBOLIC SYSTEMS

A hyperbolic system relies on ground transmitters whose accurate position is known. Two transmitters are used to obtain one position line; and two others to obtain a second position line. Where the two lines intersect is the boat's position. The two transmitters are synchronised and the times of arrival of the two transmissions are measured. If the boat is equidistant from the two transmitters, both transmissions will arrive together. If the boat is nearer one transmitter than the other, the nearest transmitter's signal will arrive first. A measurement of the difference in time between the two arrivals will therefore be a measurement of the relative distance of the two transmitters. There will be many points on the surface of the earth where there will be the same difference in time between the arrival of the two signals and, if they were joined together by a line, its shape would be a hyperbola. Having located himself on one hyperbola, the user must locate himself on another in order to get an intersection. He does this by measuring the time difference between the arrival of signals from two other transmitters. However, normally the area is covered by only three transmitters; the main or master station transmits first and triggers off the other two slave stations. They transmit after the master, but since their distance from the master is known, the delay of these transmissions is also known and this is allowed for in the receiving equipment aboard the boat. Two position lines are thus obtained: one between the master and slave A and the other between the master and slave B. The hyperbolic position lines can be drawn on a chart, but it is more usual for an onboard computer to work it all out and present the yachtsman with his position given in latitude and longitude.

DECCA
The Decca system operates in coastal waters around north-west Europe and in other local areas around the world. The effective range is 300M but this can diminish during night hours. Because of its limited range it is not suitable for ocean passage making. The accuracy is about 50m within 50M of the transmitters. The sets originally leased by Racal Decca Marine were used in conjunction with charts with a Decca lattice overlaid on them. It was relatively easy to see that where the lattice was compact the accuracy was high and as distance from the transmitter was increased the lattice pattern opened up with a consequent decrease in potential accuracy. On the base line from a master station extended beyond a slave station the lattice was very indeterminate which implied that there could be an error of more than one mile. This is not evident from sets giving a position as latitude and longitude.

LORAN-C
Loran-C has chains covering the North Atlantic, Mediterranean, Norwegian Sea, East Coast of America, North and Central Pacific, and South-East Asia with probable extensions to the North Sea and South-East Atlantic. As it utilises skywave transmission as well as groundwave transmission it has a much greater range (1,000M) than Decca. At long range, the accuracy of Loran-C is 200m, but this improves to 70m at closer distances.

Satellite navigation

For world-wide position fixing, the use of radio broadcasts from orbiting navigation satellites is by far the most effective. An early system with 5 satellites (TRANSIT) has been replaced by a system with 24 satellites (Global Positioning System or GPS) which overcomes the problem of long delays between fixes. The accuracy is potentially extremely high (16m) but for security reasons commercially available sets will have an accuracy of about 100m.

TRANSIT
A network of five satellites circle the earth at a height of 600M and an orbital time of 107 minutes. Depending on the boat's position this gives a time between fixes of 35 to 100 minutes. The receiver measures the range difference between the boat and two positions of the satellite to get one position line, then repeats the process later for a second position line. The point of intersection of these two lines (and a third if available) gives the boat's position. The range difference is obtained by measuring the doppler shift of the satellite's transmitted frequency, due primarily to the satellite's own motion, but also taking into account the boat's motion. The accuracy of the system depends on the accuracy of the input course and speed.

GLOBAL POSITIONING SYSTEM
A network of 24 satellites orbits the earth at a height of 11,000M with their orbital plane 55° to the equator. The satellites transmit continuously to earth on two frequencies in the D band (1 to 2 GHz) and supply users with their position, velocity and time. Time is obtained from three atomic clocks which are so accurate that they will gain or lose only one second in 50,000 years. The satellites have an elaborate control system. There are five ground control monitor stations located around the earth to receive technical telemetered data from the satellites. The master control station sifts all the information it receives and transmits to the satellites their own true position in space and the satellites in turn transmit their positions to the ground users.

A ship will have a two-channel receiver. To use the receiver, switch it on and enter DR position, course and speed, and ship's time. The receiver then searches for available satellites, selects the most suitable, and starts tracking them. From each such satellite it receives the satellite's position, its number and accurate time. The receiver then calculates the satellite's range by measuring the time of receipt of the signal and multiplying the time taken for the signal to come from the satellite by the speed of radio waves in air. The receiver has thus located itself on a sphere of radius R_1, whose centre is the transmitting satellite. The receiver then measures the range of the second and third satellites to define spheres of radius R_2 and R_3. The receiver can then work out the point where the spheres intersect and displays this point as latitude and longitude.

Communications

VHF RADIO TELEPHONE

Many small craft are fitted with a VHF (very high frequency) radio telephone. It is a radio transmitter/receiver that enables the skipper of such a craft to communicate with a coast radio station (connecting to the public exchange network), a port or harbour radio station, and other vessels. In particular he can communicate with the Coastguard and with marinas and yacht harbours; but, most important, he can summon assistance in distress or in an emergency. With the exception of the latter instance, any person who uses the radio for transmission must have an operator's licence or be directly supervised by a licence holder. This is because the operation of a radio telephone allows anyone to listen to any transmission: so there has to be a strict discipline controlling any transmissions. It is not difficult to learn and it is in the interest of all skippers to become qualified.

In emergency or distress it is important that *all* the crew should understand the procedures, see page 139.

The Coastguard has a VHF radio direction finder and, in *emergencies*, will inform a boat of its position.

For long distance passage making, some skippers carry emergency position indicating radio beacons (EPIRBs). When activated these transmit an alarm tone on aircraft distress frequencies which enable the distressed boat or liferaft to be located.

Chapter Sixteen

Coastal Passage: Outward Bound

We have obtained the use of a sailing boat which is lying on one of the Sailing Club moorings off Christchurch Quay. The boat's name is *Plover*. She has a length of 7.9m and a draught of 1.0m. She is sloop rigged and has an outboard engine. Her normal cruising speed under sail is 4k and under power it is 3k. On 10th July we expect to be able to get on board at 0900 and would like to sail down to Swanage to anchor, possibly staying overnight. The weather forecast is: wind south to south east force 2 to 3, weather hazy, visibility moderate.

Preparation

Study chart 15. Find Christchurch Quay and Swanage Bay noting the anchorage in the latter. With moderate visibility (5M or less) a passage along the coast would be preferred. The wind is good for sailing, though there will be a little swell at the entrance to Christchurch harbour. Extending from Hengistbury Head is Christchurch Ledge which may cause a disturbed sea but no danger in a Force 3 wind as long as Beerpan Rocks are left well clear. We will need some clearing bearings or clearing transits for this. Following the coastline westwards towards Bournemouth should present no problems; and there are some convenient yellow buoys to help with our navigation. From Bournemouth we can cross over towards the entrance to Poole Harbour, continuing towards Swanage.

The anchorage seems clear to the north west of the pier with plenty of landmarks in the town. The seabed is fine sand (fS) in the anchorage.

Tides. See Extract 3 p. 189 and Extract 4 p. 190.

Height of tide required to clear bar in the entrance channel (charted depth 0_1) will be $1.0 + 0.5 - 0.1 = 1.4$m (draught + safe clearance – charted depth). Fill in tidal curve diagram, Fig 7.7. Earliest time to cross the bar is LW + 2h 50m or 0632. The latest time to cross the bar is LW – 3h 00m or 1308: so we must clear Christchurch entrance by 1308. There are no tidal constraints at Swanage.

	LW Time	Height	HW Time	Height	LW Time	Height	Range
Portsmouth GMT	0317	1.0	1027	4.4	1543	1.0	3.4
Differences	– 0035	– 0.7		– 2.6	– 0035	– 0.7	mid
Christchurch	0242	0.3		1.8	1508	0.3	range
Add 1 hour	0100				0100		
Christchurch BST	0342				1608		

Tidal Streams. The tidal stream diagram on chart 15 refers to HW at Portsmouth and LW at Poole (Town Quay) and Portsmouth. See Extract 3 p. 189.

	LW	HW	LW	HW
Portsmouth GMT	0317	1027	1543	2247
Add 1 hour	+ 0100	+ 0100	+ 0100	+ 0100
Portsmouth BST	0417	1127	1643	2347

Average range: 3.4m which is 0.3 down from springs (Portsmouth: spring range = 4.1m, neap range = 2.0m).

The only relevant tidal diamond is B off Poole entrance. The south-going stream is from HW – 1 to HW + 4 or 1027 to 1527. The north-going stream is from HW + 5 to HW – 2 or 1627 to 2147.

To avoid the foul tide off Poole entrance, we should aim to be in Swanage Bay before 1627.

The distance from Christchurch entrance to Swanage is 13M. At a boat speed of 4k under sail the passage time will be 3h 15m, though the favourable tidal stream may reduce this period. We must be outside Christchurch entrance by 1308 and we would like to be at Swanage by 1627. If the wind is predominantly south-east force 3 (SE 3), there is no problem. If the wind dies away and the passage is made under power 3k, the passage time should not exceed 4h 20m which will just about be acceptable.

Refer to any sailing directions (see the reverse of chart 15) and yachtsmen's almanacs (see Extract 6 p. 191) for details of any local navigational information that might be relevant to the passage.

Passage

Variation 5°W used

The following is an extract from the deck log of *Plover*:

FROM: *Christchurch*   TO: *Swanage*   DATE: *10th July*

TIME		LOG	COURSE (°M)	WIND	BARO
1100	Slipped from mooring at Christchurch Quay Under power. Set courses to follow buoyed channel out of Christchurch harbour			SE 2	1024
1215	Crossed bar. Hoisted mainsail and working jib				
1230	Off Christchurch entrance. Set course 207°M. Stopped engine. Set log to zero. Leeway negligible.	0.0	207	SE 3	
1240	Established clearing bearing of 004°M on yellow buoy off groynes to keep clear of Beerpan Rocks				
1245	N end of sandbar at Christchurch entrance 012°M CG Lookout on Hengistbury Head in transit with beacon on end of groyne bearing 307°M. Altered course to 283°M	1.0	283		
1300		2.1	283	SE 3	
1303	Yellow buoy abeam. Altered course 273°M	2.2	273		
1340	Water Tower 063°M Hotel in Bournemouth 284°M Boscombe Pierhead in transit with yellow buoy 335°M	4.6	273		
1400	Yellow buoy off Bournemouth Pier abeam. Altered course 209°M	6.0	209	SE 3	1025
1421	St Peter's Church Spire 017°M Haven Hotel 265°M	7.4	209		
1445	Poole Fairway buoy 209°M Training Bank beacon 270°M East Hook buoy 323°M	9.0	209		
1458	Poole Fairway buoy abeam to stbd. Altered course 201°M	9.9	201		
1500		10.0	201	SE 3	
1504	Poole Fairway buoy 021°M Old Harry rock 295°M Altered course 209°M	10.3	209		
1522	Left hand edge of Durlston Head 209°M Swanage Methodist Church Spire 243°M Altered course 243°M	11.5	243		

FROM: *Christchurch*   TO: *Swanage*   DATE: *10th July*

TIME		LOG	COURSE	WIND	BARO
1531	*Monument on seafront in transit with Church Spire 243°M Maintained course to keep on transit Started engine. Dropped sails*				
1540	*Swanage Pierhead in transit with left hand edge of Peveril Point Altered course 123°M*	*12.4*	*123*		
1545	*Anchored off Swanage Pier, Depth of water 2.7m. 10m of anchor cable let out. Anchor bearings: Pierhead in transit with Peveril Point, end of Jetty 221°M*	*12.5*		*ESE 3*	*1026*

Having anchored at Swanage a nasty swell is beginning to build up. Also the wind is shifting towards the east and blowing straight into the anchorage. The barometer is rising rapidly which may mean that the wind strength could increase. It would be prudent to leave Swanage and go into Poole Harbour.

QUESTIONS

16.1 From the extract from *Plover*'s deck log, plot the passage on chart 15.

16.2 Plates 4 to 17 are a series of views that might have been taken during the passage. Study them in conjunction with chart 15 and try to work out the latitude and longitude of the position from which the photograph was taken. (*Note:* A 'chine' is a name used in Dorset and the Isle of Wight to define a deep narrow ravine which may appear as a marked cleft in a cliff face.)

16.3 Study Plate 18. Can you identify the central feature? At what bearing (approximately) from the central feature has the photograph been taken? If the boat, from which the photograph was taken, proceeds on a northerly course, what will happen to the central feature?

Chapter Seventeen

Coastal Passage: Inward Bound

It is 1600 on 10th July and the yacht *Plover* (described in Chapter 16) is at anchor in Swanage Bay. The wind has shifted to the east and the increasing swell is making the anchorage uncomfortable. It is decided to enter Poole Harbour, possibly going as far as Wareham.

Preparation

Study chart 15. From Swanage Bay there are no hazards northward to Poole Fairway buoy. From the Fairway buoy, the Swash Channel is well buoyed with green conical buoys to starboard and red can-shaped buoys to port. There is a chain ferry between North Haven Point and South Haven Point. Turning to starboard in front of Brownsea Castle there is a south cardinal buoy marking the division between two channels: we will take Middle Ship Channel branching to the left. On approaching Poole Town the Little Channel branches off to the right; but we will continue straight on leaving the Ro-Ro Terminal to starboard. The buoyed channel winds about a little between areas of moorings before dividing with a narrow channel to the right leading to Rockley Point. The Wareham Channel is to the left across an open expanse of water; but there is a line of red port hand buoys leading to a line of perches (thin posts). Beyond the perches is the River Frome leading to Wareham. The charted depth in several places is 0.1m (0_1). There appear to be several boatyards where there are mooring facilities for yachtsmen: Cobbs Quay Marina, Sunseekers Marina, Dorset Yacht Co, Salterns Marina, Ridge Wharf Yacht Centre and alongside the quays at Poole and Wareham.

Tides. See Chapter 16 and Tidal Information panel on chart 15. HW Portsmouth is at 2347 (BST). The range of the tide at Portsmouth is 3.4m which is about one-third (0.3) down from springs. HW at Poole (Entrance) is 3h 30m before HW Portsmouth (interpolating between

– 2h 40m at springs and – 5h 10m at neaps) which is 2017. HW at Poole (Town Quay) is 3h 00m before HW Portsmouth or 2047 at which time the height of tide will be about 2.0m above chart datum. This means that there will be a rising tide until about 2030 all the way up to Wareham and, generally, sufficient height of tide for *Plover* to clear the areas with a charted depth of 0.1m.

Tidal Streams. See Chapter 16 and chart 15. The relevant tidal diamonds are B off Poole Fairway buoy and C to H throughout the length of Poole harbour. LW at Portsmouth is at 1643 (BST). At tidal diamond F the flood tide is between LW + 30m (1713) and LW + 5 (2143). At tidal diamond C the flood tide is from LW (1643 to LW + 4 (2043). At tidal diamond B the north-going stream is from HW + 5 (1627) to HW – 2 (2147).

The distance from Swanage to Wareham is 15M. It would be reasonable to sail from Swanage until a point half way up the Swash Channel (a distance of 5M) but then it might be prudent to proceed to Wareham under power or under reduced sail (foresail only). So the time taken to reach Wareham will be: (5M at 4k plus 10M at 3k) = 4h 35m. Leaving straight away (at 1600) would mean an ETA at Wareham of 2035. As this does not include any allowance for favourable tidal stream and is well within the hours of daylight, then the timing for the passage is quite acceptable.

QUESTIONS

17.1   Using the extract from the deck log of the yacht *Plover* as shown in Chapter 16 as an example, write up a simulated deck log for the passage from Swanage to Wareham assuming a departure time of 1630, a boat speed of 4k to the chain ferry between N Haven Pt and S Haven Pt and 3k thereafter.

17.2   Using Plates 19 to 26 identify the views and work out the position from which each photograph was taken.

17.3   Plate 27 shows a view taken on the way to an alternative destination had it been decided not to proceed as far as Wareham. Identify the view.

Chapter Eighteen

Test Paper A: Navigation

Chart 15

Use variation 5°W. Times are BST and answers should be given in BST.

A1.   On 5th August a boat is sailing from Yarmouth (Isle of Wight) to the anchorage in Studland Bay. The wind is west force 4. At 1010, log 10.7, she passes the Fairway buoy off the Needles. She is on the starboard tack making good a course of 230°M with leeway estimated at 5°. At 1100, log 13.8, she tacks through 90°. At 1110, log 14.5, the following bearings are taken:

Anvil Point lighthouse	275°M
Water tower to the left of Hengistbury Head	350°M

Plot the position at 1110.

A2.   Assuming a boat speed of 4k, at what time should the boat tack in order to arrive at the Poole Fairway buoy on the next tack? What will be her ETA at the buoy? Leeway is 5°. Use tidal diamond A until 1300 then tidal diamond B.

A3.   At 1210, log 18.6, course 320°M, bearings are taken as follows:

Anvil Point lighthouse	247°M
Right hand edge of Handfast Point	281°M
Water tower	015°M

Plot the position at 1210.

A4.   At 1215 the wind starts dying away. At 1300 it is decided to motor to Studland Bay. At 1310, log 19.9, the following bearings are taken:

Left hand edge of Durlston Head	233°M
Left hand edge of Haven Hotel	305°M

Plot the position at 1310.

A5.   From the 1310 position, what is the magnetic course to steer to Poole Fairway buoy? Use tidal diamond B and a boat speed of 3k. What is the ETA at the buoy?

A6.   Steering the course from Question A5, at 1355, log 22.1, Poole Fairway buoy bears 198°M at a distance of 0.3M. What has been the direction and rate of the tidal stream between 1310 and 1355?

A7.   At 1355 the boat steers towards Poole Fairway buoy which is reached at 1405. She then alters course for the anchorage in Studland Bay. The estimated tidal stream is 290°T 0.3k. At a boat speed of 3k, what is the magnetic course to steer to the anchorage? What is the ETA? How can the boat's ground track be checked?

A8.   The boat anchors at 1420. On arrival the depth of water is measured as 4.0m. If remaining overnight, what will be the least depth of water in the anchorage and how much anchor cable should be let out? What is the quality of the bottom? Use tidal differences for Swanage and the tidal curve diagram for Christchurch.

PART 2

Chapter Nineteen

Ropework

Ropes

Ropes are used on a boat for a variety of reasons: halyards to hoist sails, sheets to pull sails in, lines to moor the boat and warps to attach to anchors. At one time they were made from natural fibres such as cotton, hemp, manila and sisal, but now they are mostly made from synthetic materials. Compared with natural fibres of the same diameter, man-made fibres are lighter and stronger but can be slippery and difficult to control.

There are several kinds of synthetic materials used in rope making:

Nylon is strong and stretches. It has good shock absorbing qualities and so is ideal for mooring lines or anchor warps.

Polyester (Terylene) is strong but has low stretching properties and can be obtained pre-stretched. It is used for halyards or sheets.

Polypropylene (Courlene) is a light buoyant rope used wherever floating line is needed, such as a dinghy painter or lifebuoy line.

Kevlar is a strong, non-stretching rope.

Ropes can be constructed in several ways: laid by twisting strands together, plaited or braided (see Fig 19.1).

However they are constructed, all ropes are subject to chafe. To help prevent this, sheets should be led over rollers, and anchor warps and mooring lines passed through a length of hose where they go through a fairlead. They should be periodically washed in fresh water and left to dry naturally. They can be damaged by heat and chemicals.

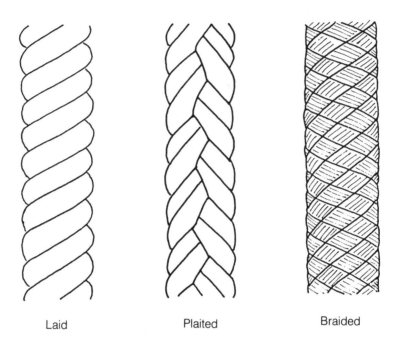

Laid   Plaited   Braided

Fig 19.1 Types of rope

Coiling rope

Ropes are normally coiled before being stowed, when preparing to come alongside or for a heaving line. (See Fig 19.2 and Plates 28 and 29.)

Heaving a line

The line is coiled and the coil divided into two, holding half in each hand as shown in Plate 29. Half the coil is swung backwards and forwards, pendulum fashion, and then thrown (heaved). The other half of the coil is allowed to run free until sufficient has run out and the end of the line has reached its target. The shore end of the line can be made heavier by tying a monkey's fist in the end as shown in Fig 19.3.

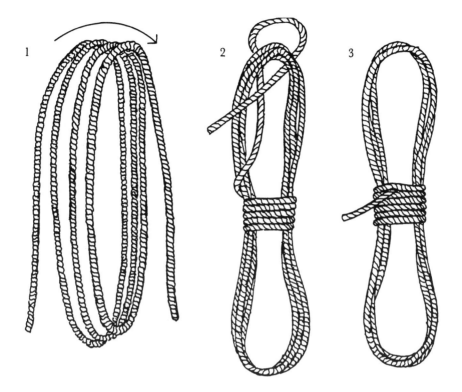

Fig 19.2 Coiling

Cable laid rope. (1) Hold the rope in the left hand and coil in a clockwise
direction. A twist at the top of each coil stops the rope twisting. (2) Bind the end
around the coils several times and then pass a loop through the coils. (3) Bring the
loop back over the top of the coils and push it down to the loops binding the coils.
Pull the end tight.

Braided or plaited rope. This type of rope twists if coiled as shown for laid rope.
It should be coiled in a figure of eight so that the twists cancel out.

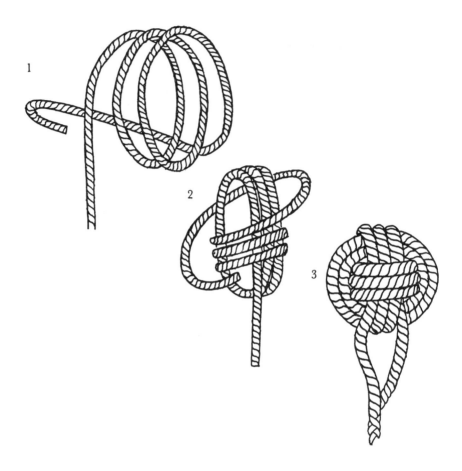

Fig 19.3 Monkey's fist. A monkey's fist is made in the end of a rope to make it heavier for heaving. Sometimes it is made around a piece of lead. (1) Make three loops. (2) Make three more loops outside the first three. (3) Make three final loops over the second three, but inside the first three and splice the end onto the standing part

29 A line coiled ready for heaving.

28 A coiled halyard hung on a cleat. After cleating a halyard, the remainder is coiled, starting from the end nearest the cleat. About one third of a metre should be left between the cleat and the coil to make a bight in the rope. This is twisted, passed through the coil and looped over the cleat.

Knots

There are many different knots; some of the most useful are shown below
(Figs 19.4–19.11).

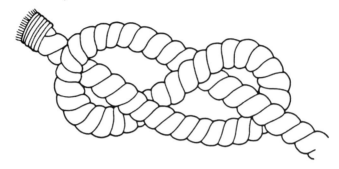

Fig 19.4 Figure of eight, sometimes called a stopper knot. It is used on the end of
a sheet to stop it accidentally pulling through a block

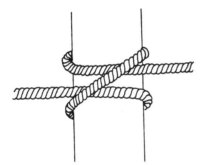

Fig 19.5 Clove hitch. Used to attach
the burgee to the burgee pole. Unless
under equal tension at both ends this
hitch will pull out, and so it is
unsuitable to use for mooring or for
securing fenders permanently

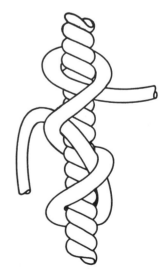

Fig 19.6 Rolling hitch. Used to fasten a rope to a
spar, a chain, or a thicker rope to temporarily
take the tension. The direction of pull should be
lengthwise across the round turn

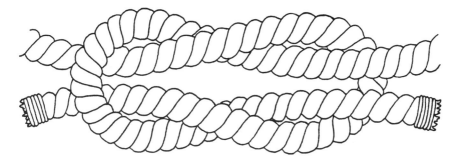

Fig 19.7 Reef knot. Used for fastening two ends of the same rope together when reefing a sail

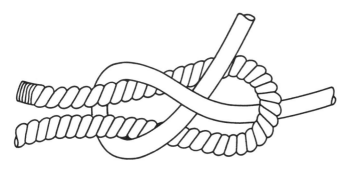

(a) Sheet bend

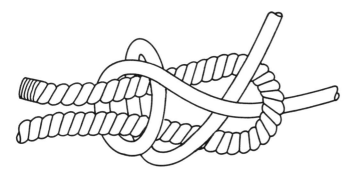

(b) Double sheet bend

Fig 19.8(a) Sheet bend. For joining two ropes together. (b) The rope can be passed through twice to make a more secure double sheet bend.

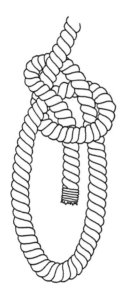

Fig 19.9 Bowline. The best all-purpose knot where a temporary loop is required. Some uses are: to fasten the sheets to the headsail; to join two ropes together; to put a temporary eye in a rope

Fig 19.10 Round turn and two half-hitches. Used for securing a line to a post or ring or for attaching fenders to the boat. It is secure but easy to undo

Fig 19.11 Fisherman's bend. For bending a warp on to the ring on an anchor. It is more secure than a round turn and two half-hitches, and holds well on slippery rope

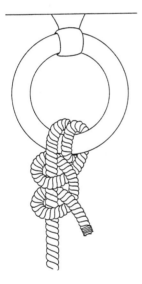

Round turn and two half hitches

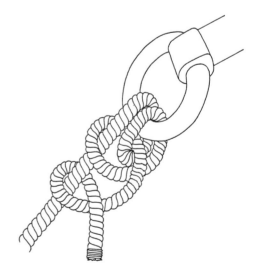

Fisherman's bend

Winching

A halyard or sheet is turned around a winch drum to take the strain when hoisting or sheeting in a sail. The most important thing to remember when winching is to keep your fingers well away from the winch when there is strain on the rope. The best way to avoid this is to turn the sheet around the winch drum in the manner shown in Plate 30, clenching your fists and keeping them well away from the winch. If the sheet has to be eased out, the palm of the hand should be used (see Plate 31).

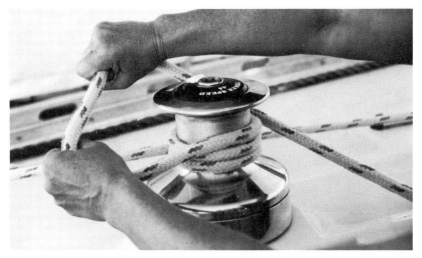

30 Turning a sheet around a winch drum. Above: Correct – the fists are clenched around the sheet and kept well away from the winch drum. Below: Incorrect – the fingers will be trapped against the winch drum.

31 Easing out a sheet. The palm of the hand is placed against the turns on the drum. The end of the sheet is held in the other hand and the sheet gradually eased out.

To release a sheet lift it above the winch and pull the turns off the top (Fig 19.12).

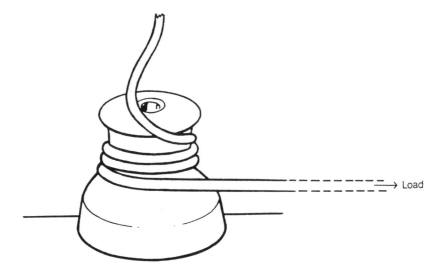

Fig 19.12 Releasing a sheet

A RIDING TURN

Sometimes one turn of a halyard or sheet on the winch drum slips over another and becomes jammed (see Plate 32); this is called a riding turn. It may occur because there are too many turns of rope on the winch drum, or because the lead on to or off the winch is not quite right. They usually free themselves but, if hopelessly jammed, another line must be attached to the halyard or sheet by a rolling hitch (see Fig 19.6) and the tension taken on this line. With the load off the winch, it is easy to remove the riding turn from the winch drum.

32 A riding turn.

Cleating

Fig 19.13 shows how a halyard is secured to a cleat. Plate 33 shows a self jamming cleat where it is only necessary to turn the rope around the cleat to secure it. This type is useful for sheets as it enables them to be released quickly.

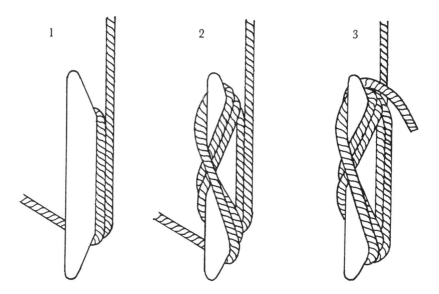

Fig 19.13 Making up a cleat. (1) Start with a turn around the cleat. (2) Follow with two or three cross turns. (3) Finish with a round turn to jam the rope

33 A self-jamming cleat.

Mooring lines

An alternative to cleating a mooring line is to make an eye on the end of the rope and drop it over a cleat or bollard. Fig 19.14 shows the lines used when mooring alongside and Fig 19.15 shows how to pass the mooring line through other boats' lines without fouling them.

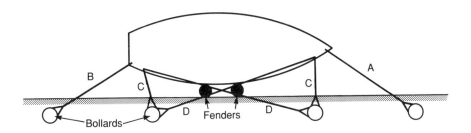

A Bow line – to keep the bow in
B Stern line – to keep the stern in
C Breast lines – to keep the boat alongside
D Spring lines – to stop the boat from surging
                       fore and aft

Fig 19.14 Mooring lines

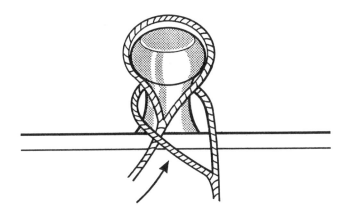

Fig 19.15 Mooring to a bollard. Pass the line under any existing ones before dropping over bollard

QUESTIONS

19.1   Which knot would be the most suitable to use in the following cases?
    a. To stop a sheet pulling through a block
    b. To secure a line to a mooring ring
    c. To make a temporary loop in a rope

19.2   What type of line would you use for:
    a. Mooring lines?
    b. Halyards?
    c. A lifebuoy line?

19.3   What do you consider to be the best all-purpose knot?

19.4   What lines would be required to berth a boat alongside in a marina?

19.5   What is the most important thing to remember when turning a sheet around a winch drum?

Chapter Twenty

Anchorwork

Anchoring is a way of preventing the boat from drifting when a temporary stop is necessary. This could be a short stop for lunch or an overnight stay in a sheltered bay.

Types of anchor

An anchor is made out of heavy metal. A length of chain or warp, or a combination of both, is attached to the anchor and to the boat. There are many different types of anchor. The principal ones are shown in Fig 20.1.

FISHERMAN

The traditional anchor is shown in Fig 20.1(a), and is sometimes called an Admiralty pattern anchor.

Advantages
1. Can be stowed flat.
2. Good holding power in sand and mud.
3. Few moving parts to get fouled up or nip fingers.

Disadvantages
1. A heavier anchor needed than some other types to give equal holding power.
2. When stowed on deck, the flukes can do damage in heavy seas unless well secured.
3. Because there is a vertical fluke when it is on the seabed, there is a possibility of the anchor chain or warp fouling this, or the boat settling on it.

121

CQR

The CQR is a proprietary type of anchor and shown in Fig 20.1(b). It is sometimes also called a plough. Imitations are often not as good.

Advantages
1. Holds well in soft sand and mud.
2. Lighter anchor required than a Fisherman to give equal holding power.
3. Usually digs in well unless the point impales a tin (filling the hollow portion with lead adds extra weight and encourages it to dig into the seabed).

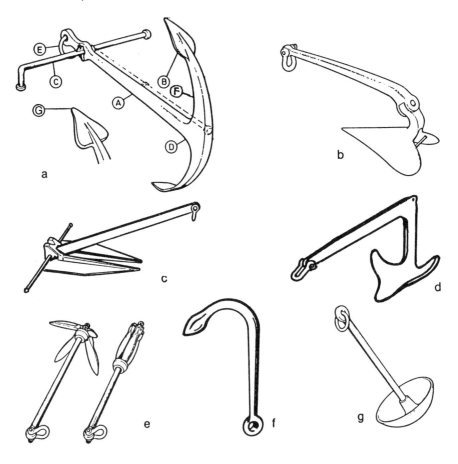

Fig 20.1 (a) Fisherman anchor; (b) CQR anchor; (c) Danforth anchor; (d) Bruce anchor; (e) Grapnel anchor (folding type); (f) Rond anchor; (g) Mushroom anchor. The parts of the Fisherman anchor are as follows: A shank, B fluke, C stock, D crown, E ring, F arm, G bill

Disadvantages
1. There may be stowage difficulties, and special chocks are needed to secure it unless fitted over the bow roller.
2. Movable parts can become fouled and damage the fingers.
3. Can capsize.
4. Can be difficult to break out of mud unless a tripping line is used.
5. Does not hold too well in kelp or hard sand.

DANFORTH

The Danforth, shown in Fig 20.1(c), is a flat twin fluke anchor with the stock built into the head.

Advantages
1. Good holding power in sand and mud.
2. Less weight needed to equal holding power compared with a Fisherman, but about equal to a CQR.
3. Can be stowed flat.

Disadvantages
1. Movable parts can become fouled and can damage the fingers.
2. Not too good on rock.
3. Can be difficult to break out of mud unless a tripping line is used.

BRUCE

Shown in Fig 20.1(d).

Advantages
1. A much lighter anchor needed to equal the holding power of the other types.
2. No movable parts.
3. Digs well into the seabed however it lies, and quickly buries itself.
4. Good holding power in sand and mud.
5. Easy to break out.

Disadvantages
1. Difficult to stow without a special chock which, due to lack of space on the foredeck, cannot always be fitted. It can, however, be stowed over the bow roller if well secured.

GRAPNEL

A good anchor to hold on rock and useful to use as a kedge; Fig 20.1(e).

ROND

A one fluke anchor used for permanent mooring, so there is no second fluke left sticking up; Fig 20.1(f).

MUSHROOM

An anchor with good holding power used for moorings; Fig 20.1(g).

KEDGE

A small version of one of the anchors described above used for temporarily anchoring (when racing), for emergencies or for assisting the main anchor.

Anchoring

Anchors hold best in mud, clay and sand; less well in hard sand, shingle or pebbles; and poorly in rock. Weed can clog movable parts, with consequent loss of holding power. Where there is rock they can become fouled and, if the rock is covered with slippery weed, they can skitter across this without holding. The Fisherman is probably the best for holding in rock. Two main anchors, preferably of different types, should be carried, together with a small kedge.

When selecting an anchorage, the following things should be considered:

1. Good holding ground free from obstructions.
2. Maximum shelter from all expected winds, and out of strong tidal streams.
3. Clear of obstructions and other boats when the boat swings round due to the tidal stream or wind.
4. A position where the boat has sufficient chain or warp for the maximum expected depth.
5. Sufficient water at low water to avoid grounding.
6. Out of areas used frequently by other boats.
7. Suitable transits or landmarks for bearings to check periodically that the boat is still in the anchored position.
8. Near a suitable landing stage if you intend to go ashore.

PREPARING THE ANCHOR

Before reaching the anchorage, both ends of the chain or warp must be made fast. The inboard end should be fastened to a fitting in the anchor locker by light line so that it is secure but can be quickly released or cut in an emergency. If chain is used, the outboard end is attached to the anchor by means of a shackle. To stop the shackle pin turning, a wire is rove through and twisted on to the shackle. This is called mousing. If warp is used it can either be secured by using a fisherman's bend or an eye can be made around a metal object called a thimble and a shackle used. It is advisable to have at least 6–10 metres of chain between anchor and warp. The heavy weight of chain gives a horizontal pull on the anchor, which is necessary if the anchor is to hold securely. The weight of the chain and elasticity of the warp also provide a damping action (Fig 20.2).

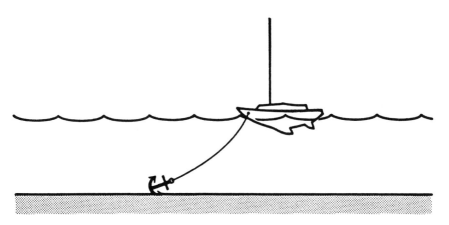

Incorrect—not enough warp or chain

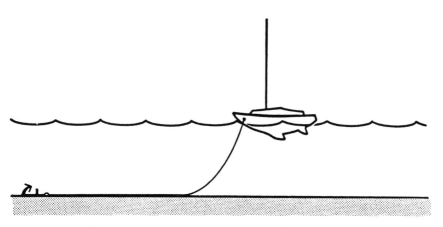

Correct—at least 4 times the
maximum depth for chain;
6 times for warp

Fig 20.2 Incorrect (*top*) and correct (*bottom*) amounts of cable. If warp is used, then at least 6 times the depth of water should be paid out. The pull on the anchor should be horizontal along the seabed to maximise the anchor's holding power. This then acts to advantage when the anchor is broken out

The required amount of chain can be laid out on deck if required, but as this can sometimes cause accidents or damage the boat, then provided it will run out freely it can be marked at 5-metre intervals and left in the anchor locker until needed.

LOWERING THE ANCHOR

When the anchorage is reached and the boat has stopped moving forward the anchor is lowered to the seabed, and as the boat falls back the required length of chain or warp is let out. If all chain is used then at least 4 times the maximum expected depth is needed; for warp allow at least 6 times; and if bad weather is expected allow at least 8 times. The inboard end of the chain or warp is temporarily made fast to a strong cleat or samson post and, when the boat is steady, transits or bearings are observed to make sure that the anchor is holding. If the anchor is dragging, more chain or warp must be let out or the anchor must be raised and the boat re-anchored. When the boat is secure the inboard end of the anchor chain or warp is made fast, as shown in Fig 20.3. The boat's position should be checked at frequent intervals and the circle through which she will swing worked out. A ball, or by night an all round white light, can be exhibited as high as possible in the fore part of the boat to show she is anchored.

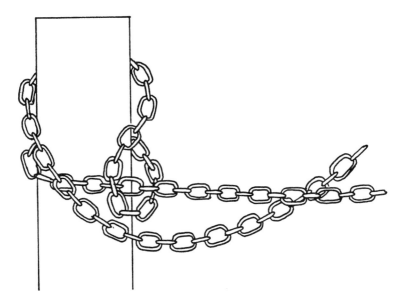

Fig 20.3 Securing the anchor cable to a samson post. The cable is turned around the post. A bight of cable is passed under the standing part and then looped back over the top of the post

Fouled anchor

If the anchor is likely to become fouled on obstructions, a trip line should be rigged (Fig 20.4). If a trip line has not been rigged and the anchor is fouled it can sometimes be freed by motoring in the direction opposite to that in which it was laid. Alternatively the chain can be hauled in until it is vertical and a separate clump of chain secured to a line which is dropped down around the original chain until it reaches the anchor, where it should slip down the shank. The inboard end of the anchor chain is buoyed and dropped into the water. The line attached to the clump of chain is then made fast to a strong cleat or post on the stern of the boat and the boat motored in the opposite direction to that in which the anchor was laid. The slightly lower point of purchase on the anchor will often drag it free.

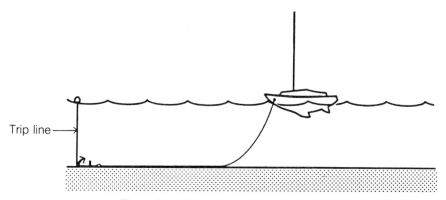

Trip line ⟶

The pull on the anchor is horizontal along the seabed.
A buoyed trip line is rigged to the crown of the anchor.

Fig 20.4 A trip line

Laying a second anchor

Sometimes it is necessary to lay a second anchor to reduce the swing or yaw of the boat due to tidal stream or strong wind, especially in a confined anchorage (the boat is then technically said to be moored). Unfortunately not all boats, because of their different hull configurations, lie at the same angle in identical conditions. Some will lie more to wind and some more to tidal stream.

One method of laying two anchors is to lead both from the bows, the heaviest one in the direction of the strongest tidal stream and the other in the opposite direction (Fig 20.5). This method is only suitable for a strong tidal stream with little or no wind. If there is a cross wind, both anchors will drag.

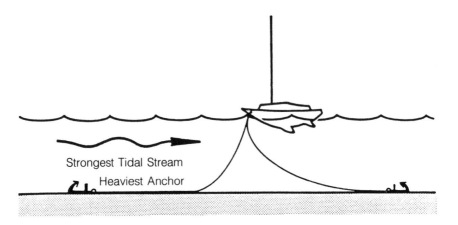

Fig 20.5 In calm conditions both anchors can be led out over the bow, the heaviest one laid towards the strongest tidal stream; but in a cross wind, both anchors may drag

Another way is to position the two anchors well forward from the bows, with not too wide an angle between them. This method is used when strong winds are expected and the boat will lie to the wind rather than to the tidal stream (Fig 20.6).

Anchoring fore and aft is not normally suitable for a small boat as it induces too much strain in a cross tide or a strong cross wind.

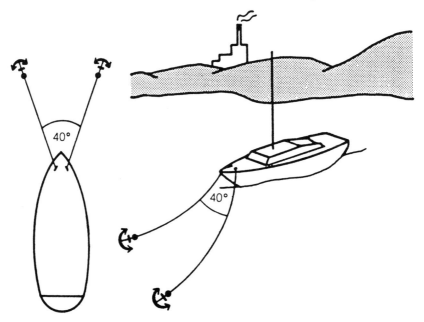

Fig 20.6 When strong winds are expected, and the boat will therefore be wind-rode and not tide-rode, both anchors can be laid from the bow, with about 40° of spread

QUESTIONS

20.1   Give two situations when a second anchor could be laid.

20.2   How does a Fisherman's anchor differ from a CQR anchor?

20.3   When is it necessary to attach a trip line to an anchor?

20.4   You intend to anchor in a sheltered bay overnight. List the considerations you would take into account.

20.5   How can you indicate to other boats that you are anchored:
a. By day?
b. By night?

Chapter Twenty-one

Safety

It is the responsibility of the skipper to ensure the safety of the boat and the crew, not only by making the right decisions at the right time, but by seeing that all personal and boat safety requirements are complied with. The following personal requirements are a necessary minimum:

1. Plenty of warm clothes and a change of clothing, including hat, gloves and towelling scarf.
2. Windproof and waterproof clothing.
3. Waterproof non-slip footwear.
4. Sharp knife.
5. Lifejacket, BS 3595, in good order.
6. Safety harness, BS 4474, in good order, preferably with two safety clips.

Personal safety

In most cases it is better to reduce the possibility of falling overboard by fastening the safety harness line to a strong point on the boat but in fog, when there is a likelihood of a collision in which the boat might sink rapidly, it may be preferable to wear a lifejacket in place of the safety harness. Additionally, lifejackets should be worn by non-swimmers, and in the dinghy to travel between the boat and the shore, as this is where a number of drownings occur. The dinghy should *never* be overloaded.

Safety harnesses should be used in rough weather (especially for foredeck work), at night or when alone at the helm. A sharp knife should always be carried (on a lanyard) to cut the safety line if necessary.

The lines on the safety harness should be too short to allow the wearer to fall in the water and be dragged along, as drowning or serious injury can occur.

With many designs of safety harness and lifejacket, it is possible to wear both at the same time and thus the choice as to which is better does not have to be made.

General safety

The amount and type of safety equipment carried depends upon the size and type of boat and its cruising area. There are recommended lists in RYA booklet C8 for craft under 13.7m (45ft). In the case of racing boats, these may be subject to special rules.

Any boat of 13.7m and over must conform to the standards laid down in the Merchant Shipping Rules; below this size the safety equipment is not compulsory but strongly recommended. A general guide is given below:

1. Liferaft of a size suitable to carry all persons on board, approved and tested to date, carried on deck where one person can quickly launch it (most liferafts are launched in cases of collision and fire, not, as one would suppose, through heavy weather).
2. A half inflated dinghy can be carried, but is a poor alternative to a liferaft and, in anything but sheltered inshore waters, is totally inadequate.
3. Lifebuoys, preferably two, one with a self-igniting light and a drogue, one with 30m of floating line attached ('U' shape is best, because this will fit under the arms of most people, whereas the ring type may not).
4. Dan buoy with self-igniting light.
5. Rescue quoit with buoyant line.
6. Boarding ladder.
7. Two strong buckets with strong handles and lanyards.
8. At least 2 multi-purpose fire extinguishers of suitable type and capacity, BS 5423.
9. Fire blanket, BS 6575.
10. Adequate efficient navigation lights of approved installation.
11. Two anchors of sufficient size, and enough chain and/or warp for all expected depths and conditions. There should be a strong point on the deck for attachment.
12. One fixed and 1 portable bilge pump.
13. An approved, up-to-date pack of flares.
14. Radar reflector.
15. First aid box.
16. Waterproof torch.
17. Safety harness anchor points, one located near the main hatch for use as the crew step into the cockpit.
18. Strong and adequate guardrails and lifelines.
19. A method of securing and releasing the hatchboards and cover from either side.
20. The name of the boat displayed on the dodgers and on a piece of canvas to display on the coachroof if necessary.

21. A method of securing all equipment such as batteries and other heavy gear liable to do damage in heavy weather.
22. Radio receiver.
23. Marine band VHF radio.
24. Radio direction finder.
25. Radio navigational system.
26. An efficient steering and hand bearing compass.
27. Reliable clock or watch.
28. Distance log.
29. Echo-sounder.
30. Lead line.
31. Up-to-date charts, sailing directions, tide tables and other relevant nautical publications.
32. Plotting instruments.
33. Tool kit.
34. Bolt croppers.
35. Engine spares.
36. A separate battery, used only for engine starting.
37. Tow rope.
38. Emergency water supply.
39. Rigid tender or inflatable dinghy.
40. A mainsail capable of being deeply reefed or a trysail, and a storm jib.

Man overboard

Sometimes, although all precautions have been taken, a person will fall overboard. An efficient method of recovery needs to be perfected both under sail and motor, which can be done by each member of the crew in all weather conditions. The preferred method will depend upon the conditions, the type of boat, the ability of the helmsman and the availability of other crew members.

Immediately a person falls overboard the following actions must be carried out:

1. The lifebuoy (and dan buoy) must be thrown in as near to the person as possible.
2. As this is being done, *Man Overboard* is shouted loudly to alert all crew members.
3. If there are sufficient crew, a lookout is appointed immediately who points to the person in the water and continuously calls out his position. (In a rough sea or at night anyone in the water is quickly lost to sight.)

The lifebuoy (and dan buoy) should have a powerful light for night use. Retro-reflective materials on all safety equipment and clothing are well worthwhile.

To help guide the helmsman to the pick up point, any buoyant object can be thrown in periodically to form a trail. If available immediately, a buoyant orange smoke canister makes a good marker for day use, or a white parachute rocket flare to illuminate the area by night.

One method of returning to the man overboard under sail is given below:

Whatever point of sailing the boat is on, she immediately goes on to a reach (wind across the boat at a right angle) and sails on for a sufficient distance to enable the boat to tack and return at a slow speed under full control. After tacking the boat reaches back, dropping slightly to leeward for the final approach which is made on a close reach with the sails flying so that the boat will stop with the person to leeward.

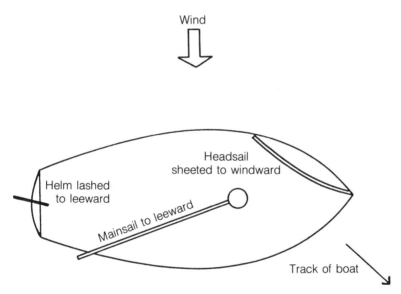

Fig 21.1 Heaving-to. The helm is lashed to leeward and the headsail sheeted to windward. The drive of the mainsail is thus counteracted

Using this method the boat is always under full control, though it is necessary to travel some distance before tacking to give the boat room to manoeuvre and stop. It is, therefore, not a good method to use at night or in a rough sea when the person in the water will be lost to sight. In this case it is better to stop the boat quickly by heaving-to to windward of the person and then drifting towards him, or motoring back to him (Fig 21.1 shows a boat hove-to). It may not be possible to bring the boat safely alongside the person in the water in heavy seas and so a rescue quoit attached to a buoyant line should be prepared ready to throw if required.

THE PICK UP

It is extremely difficult to lift a waterlogged person back on board, especially if he is unconscious. As soon as the person is alongside he should be secured to the boat so that he does not drift away. A ladder should be used for recovery, or a line in which a bowline has been tied can either be placed around his waist or hung over the side for him to step into to make recovery easier. If the person is unconscious, another crew member, who must be secured to the boat, may have to go into the water. In this case, if the dinghy is available the person in the water can be pulled into it before being winched on to the boat. Alternatively a small sail can be attached by its luff to the guardrail, lowered into the water and passed under him. A halyard is attached to the clew of this sail so that he can be hauled in over the guardrail.

AFTERCARE

Anyone who has fallen from a boat will be in a distressed condition. He may be unconscious, not breathing, suffering from shock or cardiac arrest. It is essential that all crew members are able to render first aid for these conditions and they are strongly advised to attend a recognised course.

RESUSCITATION

When breathing has stopped it is necessary to start resuscitation. Unless this is done within four minutes brain damage may occur.

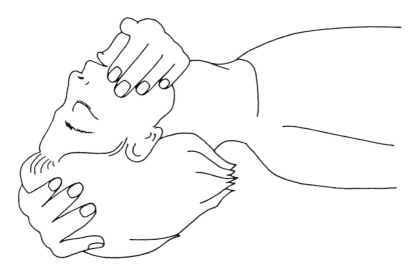

Fig 21.2 The correct position of the head for mouth-to-mouth resuscitation

Expired air resuscitation
1. Lie the patient on his back.
2. Clear his mouth of obstructions and check whether he has swallowed his tongue (but do not waste time).
3. Tilt his head back and lift his jaw as shown in Fig 21.2. This lifts the tongue away from the back of the throat and creates an open airway.
4. Pinch his nose and blow firmly into his mouth or close his mouth with your thumb and blow gently but firmly into his nose. Whichever method is used see that a good seal is made. His chest should rise; if it does not, check for obstructions.
5. Turn your head away, wait for his chest to fall, take a breath and repeat. Initially give 4 to 6 quick breaths and then one every 5 seconds.
6. Continue until he is breathing normally or until there is no hope of recovery.
7. If normal breathing is resumed, watch him carefully to see that his breathing does not fail again.

For small children and babies more rapid breathing is needed. Be careful not to blow too hard as the lungs may be damaged. If a person's heart has stopped beating, closed chest cardiac massage should be applied. This needs to have been properly learned, however, if it is to be successful.

Any person who has suffered a hit on the head and become unconscious, had severe hypothermia, or recovered from an apparent drowning should be referred to a doctor as soon as possible.

Contents of a first aid kit

The first aid kit should be kept in a watertight box and a list of the contents should be on the outside of the box. The following is a basic kit:

Roll of plaster	Calamine lotion
Individual plasters	Safety pins
Large triangular bandages	Disinfectant
Small bandages	Aspirin
Lint	Seasickness tablets
Cotton wool	Indigestion tablets
Scissors	Exposure bag
Tweezers	First aid book
Eye lotion and eye bath	

First aid has been dealt with here only briefly. During the winter months it is a good idea to attend a first aid course and learn how to administer it thoroughly.

Fire

A fire on a boat at sea can be very alarming. If the fire looks as though it might get out of hand, prepare to abandon ship. Get the dinghy inflated and tow it astern. See that the liferaft is ready to launch immediately. Don lifejackets and then standby to initiate distress procedures.

The best way to deal with a fire is to smother it (thus starving it of oxygen) and prevent it spreading by cooling the surrounding areas.

The number and type of extinguishers to be carried on a boat depend upon the type and size of the boat. For extinguishers made to BS 5423, capacity is expressed as a number, whilst the type is shown by a letter. The letter A denotes an extinguisher suitable for fires caused by paper, wood etc; B is for burning liquids such as oil and fuel; whilst C is for flammable gasses. Most extinguishers deal with at least two types of fire. A minimum requirement for a boat fitted with a galley and engine is 2 multi-purpose extinguishers with a fire rating of 5A/34B. Fire authorities recommend that one 13A/113B should also be carried. Fire extinguishers should be stowed in a readily accessible place and maintained regularly.

Water may be used on non-oil, non-electric fires such as bedding. A bedding fire may appear to be extinguished but can often smoulder and restart, so plenty of water must be used. This type of fire is often caused by someone smoking below deck.

A fire blanket is useful for cooker fires. A burning frying pan must not be thrown overboard as there is a possibility of spillage and thus spreading the fire. It should be smothered with a fire blanket, which should be applied over the fire away from the person holding it so that the flames are not fanned towards them. A heavy piece of damp material can also be used.

To help prevent fire occurring, bilges should be kept clean and well ventilated so that gas fumes do not accumulate. Gas bottles should be outside the cockpit where any leaks will drain overboard and not into the bilges. They should be turned off at the bottle when not in use. The gas in the pipes can be burned out by turning the gas off at the bottle before turning it off at the cooker.

The engine compartment should be closed when refuelling and if any fuel spillage occurs the boat should be hosed down and ventilated.

The liferaft

Everyone on board should know how to inflate and board the liferaft.

LAUNCHING

Do not launch the liferaft until the last minute as it may capsize in rough weather. Do not leave the boat if it is still afloat: abandoned boats have been found still floating with no survivors.

1. Make sure that the liferaft's painter is secured to a strong point on the boat before it is launched.
2. Release the fastening which secures the raft to the boat and launch it.
3. When it is in the water take up the slack on the painter and then tug sharply: this should inflate the raft.

BOARDING

1. Do not jump into the raft.
2. Get the heaviest person in first to stabilise it.
3. When everyone is aboard, cut the painter and paddle away from the boat.
4. Stream the drogue.
5. Elect a leader.
6. Take seasickness tablets.
7. Check for leaks.
8. Locate first aid kit, flares, repair kit, survival kit.
9. Do not issue drinking water for 24 hours unless anyone is injured and bleeding.
10. Do not drink sea water or urine.
11. Keep warm.
12. Keep a lookout and try to estimate your position.

Pyrotechnics

RED FLARES

A red handflare (pinpoint flare) is for use when within sight of land or another boat, or to pinpoint your position when the rescuers are within visible range. It burns for 1 minute. Do not point it into the wind or you will be covered with sparks and smoke. Do not look directly at it.

A parachute rocket flare is for use when out of sight of land to raise the alarm. It burns for 40 seconds and projects a very bright red parachute suspended flare to a height of 300 metres. A rocket turns towards the wind and so should be fired vertically, or in strong winds 15 degrees downwind. If there is low cloud it should be fired 45 degrees downwind so that it ignites below the cloud base.

ORANGE SMOKE FLARE

This is a daytime distress signal which produces a dense cloud of orange smoke easily seen from the air. In strong winds, however, the smoke blows along the sea surface and may not be visible from the shore or other boats. Handsmokes burn for 50 seconds and are used when rescuers are within visible range. Buoyant smokes, which consist of a container with a ring pull, can be thrown into the water and burn for 3 minutes.

WHITE HANDFLARE

This is not used for distress but to warn other boats of your position. It burns for 50 seconds. Do not look directly at it as it is very bright. White parachute flares are also available. These are generally used for demonstration purposes. They are very useful to illuminate the area in a man overboard situation.

MINIMUM RECOMMENDED PACKS

Coastal waters up to 7 miles from land:

  2 red parachute rockets
  2 red handflares
  2 handheld orange smokes

Offshore over 7 miles from land:

  4 red parachute rockets
  4 red handflares
  2 buoyant orange smokes

For collision warning:

  4 white handflares

FLARE SAFETY

1. Learn the purpose of the pyrotechnics carried and how to use them.
2. Read and memorise the operating instructions on the flares and always follow these instructions EXACTLY.
3. Stow flares in a secure, cool dry place which is easily accessible and make sure that all crew members know where this is.
4. Always have at least the minimum required number and type of pyrotechnics on board, and make sure they are within their use-by date.
5. If a signal fails, hold it in the firing position for at least 30 seconds. Remove the caps and drop it into the sea.
6. Never point pyrotechnics at another person.

VHF radio telephony

The Coastguard Maritime Rescue Centres are listed on the back of chart 15. The distress (MAYDAY) procedure used on VHF radio telephone Channel 16 is as follows:

Select Channel 16 and switch on. Check that no other transmissions are taking place. Operate the press-to-speak switch (usually on the handset). Use the following *exact* broadcast procedure:

1. Distress call (3 times)	MAYDAY MAYDAY MAYDAY
2. Callsign of boat (3 times)	THIS IS JETTO JETTO JETTO
3. Distress call	MAYDAY
4. Callsign of boat	JETTO
5. Position	ONE FIVE ZERO BEACHY HEAD LIGHT ONE POINT FIVE MILES
6. Nature of distress	STRUCK FLOATING OBJECT AND SINKING
7. Assistance required	REQUIRE LIFEBOAT
8. Other information	FOUR PERSONS ON BOARD
9. End of message	OVER

The sender may receive an immediate reply or acknowledgement from another ship, Coast Radio Station or Coastguard. If no reply is received, check that the radio is correctly switched on and tuned, then repeat the entire message at regular intervals. Once a reply is received and communication established, pass further information preceding each message with 'Mayday'. The position of the vessel is of vital importance. Do not give an apparently accurate position unless it is known to be so.

A vessel may initiate a distress call for another if the latter has no means of indicating her plight.

If a vessel receives a distress message she should listen for an acknowledgement by a Coast Radio Station or Coastguard. If this acknowledgement is not forthcoming and assistance can be rendered, then receipt should be acknowledged. If assistance cannot be rendered, then all steps must be taken to pass on the message to someone who can. The message must be preceded by the words 'Mayday Relay'.

QUESTIONS

21.1 When should a safety harness be worn?

21.2 What should you do immediately a person falls overboard?

21.3 What precautions should be taken to minimise the risk of fire?

21.4 What is the recommended flare pack for a boat in coastal waters within 7 miles of the coast?

21.5 You are in motor boat *Jetto*, which is about to sink. There are 3 other crew members as well as yourself on board. The boat is 3 miles south-west of the Needles lighthouse. Write down the appropriate VHF call you would send and state the channel on which you would send it.

Chapter Twenty-two

International Regulations for Preventing Collisions at Sea

It is absolutely necessary to have a sound knowledge of all collision rules, and this chapter should be read in conjunction with a copy of International Regulations for Preventing Collisions At Sea.

Extracts of the Convention on the International Regulations for Preventing Collisions at Sea, 1972 are reprinted by permission of IMO.

Steering and sailing rules 5, 7, 8, 9 and 12 to 19

RULE 5 LOOK-OUT

Every vessel shall at all times maintain a proper look-out by sight and hearing as well as by all available means appropriate in the prevailing circumstances and conditions so as to make a full appraisal of the situation and of the risk of collision.

It is very easy in bad weather when there is a lot of spray, especially at night, to be blind to things forward of the boat. There is also a temptation, when self steering is used, to abandon the helm. It is vital in both of these situations that a good and adequate look-out is kept. In fog, when visibility is lost, a good hearing watch should be kept. At night the helmsman may be temporarily blinded by thoughtless use of the cabin lights or matches struck close to him.

RULE 7 RISK OF COLLISION

(d) *In determining if risk of collision exists the following considerations shall be among those taken into account:*
    (i) *such risk shall be deemed to exist if the compass bearing of an approaching vessel does not appreciably change;* (ii) *such risk may sometimes exist even when an appreciable bearing change is evident, particularly when approaching a very large vessel or a tow or when approaching a vessel at close range.*

RULE 8 ACTION TO AVOID COLLISION

(a) Any action taken to avoid collision shall, if the circumstances of the case admit, be positive, made in ample time and with due regard to the observance of good seamanship.

(b) Any alteration of course and/or speed to avoid collision shall, if the circumstances of the case admit, be large enough to be readily apparent to another vessel observing visually or by radar; a succession of small alterations of course and/or speed should be avoided.

A small alteration of course by the give-way vessel may not be seen by the other vessel, a series of small alterations will be confusing, possibly causing a collision. Any alterations to be made should be bold and made in plenty of time.

RULE 9 NARROW CHANNELS

(a) A vessel proceeding along the course of a narrow channel or fairway shall keep as near to the outer limit of the channel or fairway which lies on her starboard side as is safe and practicable.

(b) A vessel of less than 20 metres in length or a sailing vessel shall not impede the passage of a vessel which can safely navigate only within a narrow channel or fairway.

(c) A vessel engaged in fishing shall not impede the passage of any other vessel navigating within a narrow channel or fairway.

(d) A vessel shall not cross a narrow channel or fairway if such crossing impedes the passage of a vessel which can safely navigate only within such channel or fairway. The latter vessel may use the sound signal prescribed in Rule 34 (d) if in doubt as to the intention of the crossing vessel.

(e) (i) In a narrow channel or fairway when overtaking can take place only if the vessel overtaken has to take action to permit safe passage, the vessel intending to overtake shall indicate her intention by sounding the appropriate signal prescribed in Rule 34 (c) (i). The vessel to be overtaken shall, if in agreement, sound the appropriate signal prescribed in Rule 34 (c) (ii) and take steps to permit safe passing. If in doubt she may sound the signals prescribed in Rule 34 (d). (ii) This Rule does not relieve the overtaking vessel of her obligation under Rule 13.

(f) A vessel nearing a bend or an area of a narrow channel or fairway where other vessels may be obscured by an intervening obstruction shall navigate with particular alertness and caution and shall sound the appropriate signal prescribed in Rule 34 (e).

(g) Any vessel shall, if the circumstances of the case admit, avoid anchoring in a narrow channel.

As no definition of a 'narrow channel' is given, the appropriate action depends upon the type and size of vessels using the channel.

Generally speaking, there is usually enough depth of water for a sailing vessel to navigate outside a buoyed channel used by deep draught vessels.

RULE 12 SAILING VESSELS

(a) *When two sailing vessels are approaching one another, so as to involve risk of collision, one of them shall keep out of the way of the other as follows:*

   (i) *When each has the wind on a different side, the vessel which has the wind on the port side shall keep out of the way of the other;*

   (ii) *When both have the wind on the same side, the vessel which is to windward shall keep out of the way of the vessel which is to leeward;*

   (iii) *If a vessel with the wind on the port side sees a vessel to windward and cannot determine with certainty whether the other vessel has the wind on the port or on the starboard side, she shall keep out of the way of the other.*

The boat to windward may have a large sail such as a spinnaker blanketing a view of the other sails. In this rule the give way boat is on port tack, and, as she cannot determine which tack the other boat is on, it must be assumed that it is on starboard and has right of way. Had the leeward boat been on starboard tack she would have held her course and speed as the windward rule (ii) would have applied (Fig 22.1).

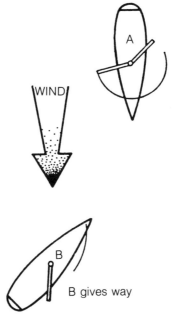

Fig 22.1 Rule 12(iii) Sailing Vessels. Because vessel B cannot clearly see which tack vessel A is on (the spinnaker blocks her view of A's mainsail) she must assume that A is on starboard, and B therefore has to give way, since she is on port tack. Had B been on starboard tack, she would hold her course under Rule 12(ii)

RULE 13 OVERTAKING

(a) *Notwithstanding anything contained in the Rules of this section, any vessel overtaking any other shall keep out of the way of the vessel being overtaken.*

The rule states *any* vessel overtaking, which is one of several instances when sail gives way to power. The give-way vessel must continue on her course until she is past and clear. As she is overtaking, the situation could go on for a long time (though it may seem to change; if a sailing boat overtakes a small motor boat and the wind suddenly dies so that the two are abreast, and then the motor boat again goes ahead, the sailing boat is *still* the give-way vessel).

RULE 14 HEAD-ON SITUATION

(a) *When two power driven vessels are meeting on reciprocal or nearly reciprocal courses so as to involve risk of collision each shall alter her course to starboard so that each shall pass on the port side of the other* (Fig 22.2(a)).

RULE 15 CROSSING SITUATION

When two power driven vessels are crossing so as to involve risk of collision, the vessel which has the other on her own starboard side shall keep out of the way and shall, if the circumstances of the case admit, avoid crossing ahead of the other vessel (Fig 22.2(b)).

The give-way vessel should alter course to starboard and pass astern of the other vessel unless she is prevented from doing so, in which case an alteration to port will have to be made which will need to be considerable if she is to avoid crossing ahead.

RULE 16 ACTION BY GIVE-WAY VESSEL

Every vessel which is directed to keep out of the way of another vessel shall, so far as possible, take early and substantial action to keep well clear.

An early alteration of course and a bold one so that the intentions of the give-way vessel are clear in good time.

RULE 17 ACTION BY STAND-ON VESSEL

(a) (i) *Where one of two vessels is to keep out of the way the other shall keep her course and speed.*
(ii) *The latter vessel may however take action to avoid collision by her manoeuvre alone, as soon as it becomes apparent to her that the vessel required to keep*

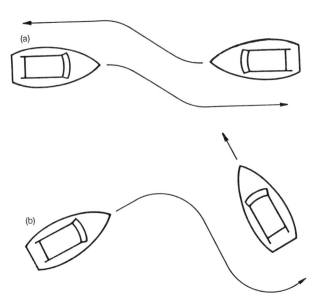

Fig 22.2 (a) Rule 14 says that power-driven vessels meeting head on shall both turn to starboard. (b) Rule 15, power-driven vessels crossing. The old ditty 'If to starboard Red appear, 'tis your duty to keep clear' helps to remember this rule

out of the way is not taking appropriate action in compliance with these Rules.
(b) *When from any cause, the vessel required to keep her course and speed finds herself so close that collision cannot be avoided by the action of the give-way vessel alone, she shall take such action as will best aid to avoid collision.*
(c) *A power-driven vessel which takes action in a crossing situation in accordance with sub-paragraph (a) (ii) of this Rule to avoid collision with another power-driven vessel shall, if the circumstances of the case admit, not alter course to port for a vessel on her own port side.*
(d) *This Rule does not relieve the give-way vessel of her obligation to keep out of the way.*

In Fig 22.3 vessel A has right of way but is not sure whether vessel B will take avoiding action. If vessel A decides that she must alter course to avoid collision and does so to port, B may suddenly decide that as give-way vessel she will take avoiding action, and if she also alters course to port to pass behind A a collision will result. A better course of action for A if she must take avoiding action would be to stop or go astern, or turn to starboard.

RULE 18 RESPONSIBILITIES BETWEEN VESSELS

Except where Rules 9, 10 and 13 otherwise require:
(a) *A power-driven vessel underway shall keep out of the way of:*
  (i) *a vessel not under command;*
  (ii) *a vessel restricted in her ability to manoeuvre;*

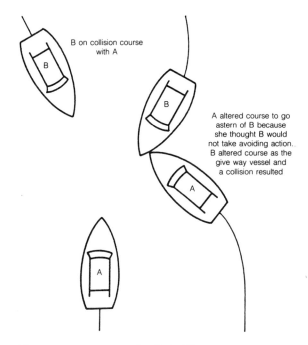

B on collision course with A

A altered course to go astern of B because she thought B would not take avoiding action. B altered course as the give way vessel and a collision resulted

Fig 22.3 How things can go wrong under Rule 17

    (iii) *a vessel engaged in fishing;*
    (iv) *a sailing vessel.*
(b) *A sailing vessel underway shall keep out of the way of:*
    (i) *a vessel not under command;*
    (ii) *a vessel restricted in her ability to manoeuvre;*
    (iii) *a vessel engaged in fishing.*
(c) *A vessel engaged in fishing when underway shall, so far as possible, keep out of the way of:*
    (i) *a vessel not under command;*
    (ii) *a vessel restricted in her ability to manoeuvre.*
(d) (i) *Any vessel other than a vessel not under command or a vessel restricted in her ability to manoeuvre shall, if the circumstances of the case admit, avoid impeding the safe passage of a vessel constrained by her draught, exhibiting the signals in Rule 28;*
    (ii) *A vessel constrained by her draught shall navigate with particular caution having full regard to her special condition.*
(e) *A seaplane on the water shall, in general, keep well clear of all vessels and avoid impeding their navigation. In circumstances, however, where risk of collision exists, she shall comply with the Rules of this Part.*

Sailing vessels must also keep clear when they are the overtaking vessel whether they are overtaking power or sail, and must not impede any vessel which has a deep draught and cannot navigate outside her channel.

    The signals (in Rule 28) exhibited by a vessel constrained by her draught are: three all round red lights in a vertical line, or a cylinder.

RULE 19 CONDUCT OF VESSELS IN RESTRICTED VISIBILITY

(a) *This Rule applies to vessels not in sight of one another when navigating in or near an area of restricted visibility.*

(b) *Every vessel shall proceed at a safe speed adapted to the prevailing circumstances and conditions of restricted visibility. A power-driven vessel shall have her engines ready for immediate manoeuvre.*

(c) *Every vessel shall have due regard to the prevailing circumstances and conditions of restricted visibility when complying with the Rules of Section 1 of this Part.*

(d) *A vessel which detects by radar alone the presence of another vessel shall determine if a close-quarter situation is developing and/or risk of collision exists. If so, she shall take avoiding action in ample time, provided that when such action consists of an alteration of course, so far as possible the following shall be avoided:*

(i) *an alteration of course to port for a vessel forward of the beam, other than for a vessel being overtaken.*

(ii) *an alteration of course towards a vessel abeam or abaft the beam.*

(e) *Except where it has been determined that a risk of collision does not exist, every vessel which hears apparently forward of her beam the fog signal of another vessel, or which cannot avoid a close-quarters situation with another vessel forward of her beam, shall reduce her speed to the minimum at which she can be kept on her course. She shall if necessary take all her way off and in any event navigate with extreme caution until the danger of collision is over.*

Great care is necessary by small boats caught in fog (see Chapter 13).

QUESTIONS

22.1   What are you required to do at all times?

22.2   If you are required to alter course to avoid another boat, what three things should you do?

22.3   Study these sketches and state which boat has right of way:

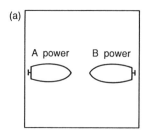
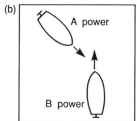
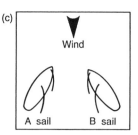

22.4   Give three instances when a sailing boat must keep clear of a motor boat.

22.5   How can you determine whether there is a risk of collision with another boat?

Chapter Twenty-three

Parts of the Boat, Nautical Terms and Definitions

Fig. 23.1(a) and (b) shows parts of the boat and Fig 23.2 shows parts of the sail.

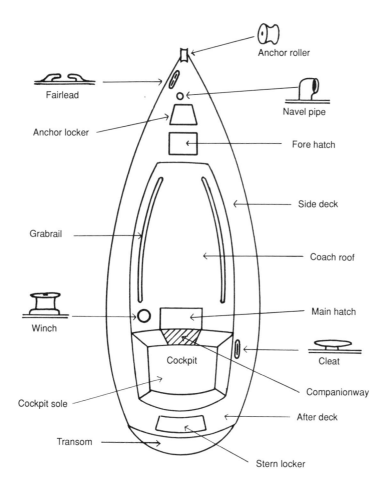

Fig 23.1 (a) Parts of the boat

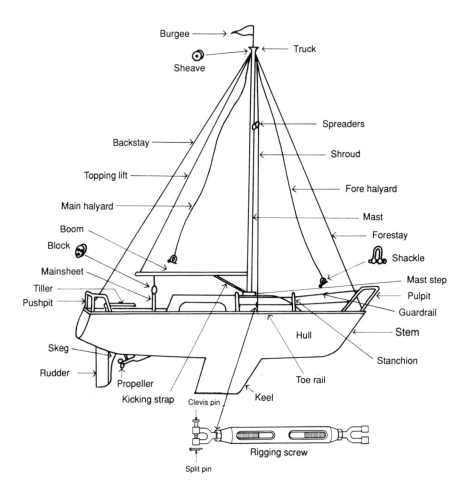

Fig 23.1 (b) Parts of the boat

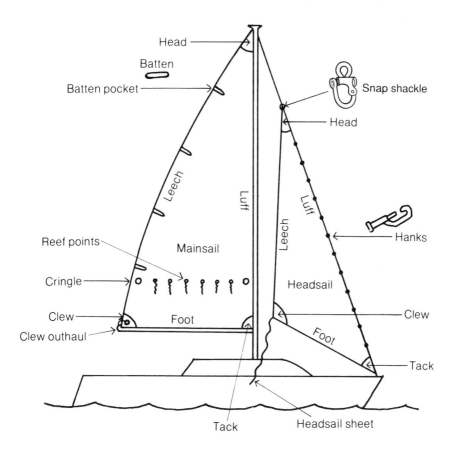

Fig 23.2 Parts of the saii

Nautical Terms and Definitions

Aback: A sail is aback when the wind strikes it on what would normally be its lee side.

Abaft the beam: The sector on both sides of a boat from abeam to astern.

Abeam: The direction at right angles to the fore-and-aft line.

Abate: The true wind abates or moderates when it blows less strongly than before.

Adrift: Not attached to the sea-bed.

Afloat: Floating; at sea.

Aft: Near or towards the stern.

Ahead: The direction of an object beyond the stem of a boat.

Ahoy: Shout to attract attention of another vessel.

Alee: To leeward.

Almanac: An annual publication containing information on, for example, buoyage, tides, signals, glossaries, and positions of heavenly bodies.

Aloft: Above deck.

Amidships: The centre part of the boat.

Anchor buoy: Buoy or float secured by a tripping line to the crown of the anchor.

Anchor cable: Chain or rope connection between a boat and her anchor.

Anchor light: An all round white light usually shackled to the forestay of a boat and hoisted to a suitable height by the jib halyard.

Anchor locker: A locker where the anchor and anchor chain are kept.

Anchor roller: A roller over which the anchor cable is passed when at anchor.

Anchor watch: Watch kept when a boat is at anchor to check whether the anchor is dragging.

Anchor well: *See* anchor locker.

Answer the helm: A boat answers the helm when she alters course in response to the helmsman's deflection of the rudder.

Apparent wind: The wind felt by the crew in a boat that is moving over the ground.

Ashore: On the land; or aground.

Astern: Direction beyond the stern; or a movement through the water in that direction.

Athwartships: At right angles to the centreline of the boat inside the boat.

Autopilot: Equipment that allows the boat to follow automatically a compass course or a course relative to wind direction.

Auxiliary: A term for a sailing boat that has auxiliary power, i.e. an engine.

Avast: Order to stop an activity.

Awash: Level with the surface of the water which just washes over an object.

Babystay: An inner forestay.

Back: To back a sail: it is sheeted or held to windward so that the wind strikes it on the side which is normally to leeward. Of wind: it backs when it shifts to blow from a direction that is further anti-clockwise.

Back splice: The end of a rope that has been finished by unlaying the strands, making a crown knot and tucking the strands back down the rope.

Backstay: A stay that supports the mast from aft.

Backwind: Airflow that is deflected on to the lee side of a sail, such as a jib backwinding the mainsail.

Bail: To remove water from the bilges or cockpit.

Bailer: A utensil used to bail water out of a boat.

Ball: A black signal shape normally displayed by day when a boat is at anchor.

Ballast: Additional weight placed low in the hull to improve stability.

Bar: A shoal close by a river mouth or harbour entrance; a measure of barometric pressure usually noted as 1000 millibars.

Bare poles: No sails are set and the boat is driven by the force of the wind on the spars and rigging.

Barnacle: A marine crustacean that attaches itself to the bottom of a boat.

Batten: A flexible strip of wood or plastic used to stiffen the leech of a mainsail.

Batten pocket: A pocket on the leech of a mainsail to contain a batten.

Beach: To run a boat ashore deliberately.

Beacon: A mark erected on land or on the bottom in shallow waters to guide or warn shipping.

Beam: The breadth of a boat.

Beam reach: A point of sailing with the wind roughly at right angles to the fore-and-aft line.

Bear: The direction of an object from an observer.

Bear away: To put the helm to windward so that the boat alters course to leeward away from the wind.

Bearing: The direction of an object from an observer given as an angle from a line of reference (true north or magnetic north).

Bearings (3 figure notation): Bearings and courses are given in a 3 figure notation, that is: 180°C or 180°T depending on whether it is a Compass or True bearing.

Beating: Sailing towards an objective to windward following a zigzag course on alternate tacks.

Beaufort scale: A scale for measurement of the force of the wind.

Belay: To make fast a line round a cleat or bollard.

Bell: In restricted visibility a bell is rung to indicate that a boat is at anchor or aground.

Below deck: Beneath the deck.

Bend: To connect two ropes with a knot; to prepare a sail for hoisting, a type of knot.

Berth: A place where a boat can lie for a period; a sleeping place on a boat; to give an obstruction a wide berth by keeping well clear.

Bight: A loop or curve in a rope or line.

Bilge: The rounded part of a boat where the bottom curves upwards towards the sides.

Bilges: The lowest part inside the hull below the cabin sole where bilge water collects.

Bilge keel: One of two keels fitted on either side of a boat's hull to resist rolling and provide lateral resistance.

Binnacle: Strong housing to protect the steering compass.

Blanket: To take the wind from another boat's sails.

Blast (foghorn): A sound signal – a short blast lasts 1 second, a prolonged blast 4 to 6 seconds.

Block: A pulley made of wood, metal or plastic.

Boat-hook: A pole, generally of wood or light alloy, with a hook at one end, used for picking up moorings and buoys.

Bollard: Strong fitting, firmly bolted to the deck, to which mooring lines are made fast. Large bollards are on quays, piers and pontoons.

Bolt rope: Rope sewn to one or more edges of a sail either to reinforce the sides or so that the sail can be fed into a grooved spar.

Boom: Spar that supports the foot of the sail.

Boom out: On a run to thrust the genoa out to windward so that it fills with wind.

Boot top: A narrow strip just above the waterline between the bottom and side of the hull. Usually of contrasting colour.

Bottlescrew: A rigging screw to tension the standing rigging or guardrails.

Bow: The forward part of a boat. A direction 45° either side of right ahead.

Bowline: A knot tied in the end of a line to make a loop that will neither slip nor jam.

Breakwater: A structure to protect a harbour or beach from the force of the sea.

Breast rope: A mooring line that runs at right angles to the centreline; one runs from the bow and another from the stern to the shore or a boat alongside.

Breather: A pipe fitted to a water or fuel tank which allows air to escape.

Broach: With heavy following seas the boat can slew round uncontrollably, heeling dangerously.

Broad reach: The point of sailing between a beam reach and a run.

Broken out: The anchor, when pulled out of the seabed by heaving on the cable, is broken out.

Bulkhead: A vertical partition below decks.

Bunk: A built-in sleeping place.

Buoy: A floating object used to indicate the position of a channel, wreck, danger, etc., or the position of an object on the seabed.

Buoyancy aid: A life-preserver to help a person float if he falls in; less effective than a lifejacket.

Burgee: A triangular flag worn at the masthead.

Cabin: The sheltered area in which the crew live and sleep.

Cable: Chain or rope that is made fast to the anchor. A measure of distance equivalent to one tenth of a nautical mile.

Capsize: The boat overturns.

Cast off: To let go a rope or line.

Cavita line: A decorative line of contrasting colour on the hull of the boat, near the rubbing strake.

Centreboard: A board lowered through a slot in the keel to reduce leeway by providing lateral resistance.

Chafe: Damage or wear resulting from friction.

Chain locker: *See* anchor locker.

Chainplate: A fitting which is bolted to the hull, to which the shrouds are attached.

Chandler: A shop which sells nautical gear.

Channel: A waterway through shoals, rivers or harbours.

Chart: Printed map giving many details about the area covered by water and details about the adjacent land.

Chart datum: Reference level on charts and for use in tidal predictions.

Clear: To disentangle a line; to avoid a danger or obstruction; improved weather.

Cleat: A fitting with two horns round which a rope is secured.

Clevis pin: A locking pin with an eye at one end through which a split ring is fitted to prevent accidental withdrawal.

Clew: The after lower corner of a sail to which the sheets are fitted.

Clew outhaul: The line which tensions the foot of the mainsail.

Close hauled: The point of sailing when the boat is as close to the wind as she can lie with advantage in working to windward.

Coachroof: The part of the cabin that is raised above the deck to provide height in the cabin.

Coaming: Vertical structure surrounding a hatch or cockpit to prevent water entering.

Coast radio station: A radio station for communication between ships at sea and the public telephone network.

Coastguard: The organisation responsible for search and rescue operations in UK waters.

Cocked hat: In navigation the triangle formed when three position lines fail to meet at a single point.

Cockpit: A space lower than deck level in which the crew can sit or stand.

Collision course: The course of a boat which, if maintained relative to that of another, would result in a collision.

Compass rose: A circle printed on a chart representing the true compass and graduated clockwise from 0° to 360°.

Cone: A signal shape displayed either point upwards or point downwards.

Counter: Above the waterline where the stern extends beyond the rudder post forming a broad afterdeck abaft the cockpit.

Course: The direction in which the boat is being, or is to be, steered.

Courtesy ensign: The national flag of the country being visited by a foreign boat; it should be flown from the starboard spreader.

CQR anchor: A patented anchor with good holding power.

Cringle: A rope loop, usually with a metal thimble, worked in the edge of a sail.

Crutch: A U-shaped fitting with a pin, which fits into a hole in the gunwale and provides a fulcrum for the oar.

Dan buoy: A temporary mark to indicate a position, say, of a man overboard. A flag flies from a spar passing through a float weighted at the bottom.

Deck log: A book in which all matters concerning navigation are entered.

Depth sounder: *See Echo-sounder.*

Deviation: The deflection of the needle of a magnetic compass caused by the proximity of ferrous metals, electrical circuits or electronic equipment.

Diaphone: A powerful two-tone fog signal with a grunt at the end.

Dip the ensign: To lower the ensign briefly as a salute. It is not rehoisted until the vessel saluted has dipped and rehoisted hers in acknowledgement.

Direction finder: A radio receiver with a directional antenna with which the bearing of a radio beacon can be found.

Displacement: The weight of a boat defined as the weight of water displaced by that boat.

Distance made good: The distance covered over the ground having made allowance for tidal stream and leeway.

Dividers: Navigational instrument for measuring distances on charts.

Dodger: Screen fitted to give the crew protection from wind and spray.

Dolphin: A mooring post or group of piles.

Double up: To put out extra mooring lines when a storm is expected.

Douse: To lower a sail or extinguish a light quickly.

Downhaul: A rope or line with which an object such as a spar or sail is pulled down.

Downstream: The direction towards which the stream flows.

Downwind: Direction to leeward.

Drag: The anchor drags when it fails to hold and slides over the seabed.

Draught: The vertical distance from the lowest part of the keel to the waterline.

Dredger: A vessel for dredging a channel.

Dress ship: On special occasions ships in harbour or at anchor dress overall with International Code flags from the stem to the top of the mast and down to the stern.

Drift: To be carried by the tidal stream. The distance that a boat is carried by the tidal stream in a given time.

Drifter: A fishing vessel that lies to her nets.

Drop astern: To fall astern of another boat.

Drop keel: A keel that can be drawn up into the hull.

Ease out: To let a rope out gradually.

Ebb: The period when the tidal level is falling.

Echo-sounder: An electronic depth-finding instrument.

Ensign: The national flag worn at or near the stern of a boat to indicate her nationality.

EPIRB: An Emergency Position Indicating Radio Beacon that transmits a distinctive signal on a distress frequency.

Even keel: A boat floating so that her mast is more or less vertically upright.

Eye: A loop or eye splice. The eyes of a boat: right forward.

Eyelet: A small hole in a sail with a metal grommet through which lacing is passed.

Eye splice: A permanent eye spliced in the end of a rope or wire rope.

Fair: Advantageous or favourable, as of wind or tide.

Fairlead: The lead through which a working line is passed in order to alter the direction of pull.

Fairway: The main channel in a body of water such as an estuary or river.

Fender: Any device hung outboard to absorb the shock when coming alongside and to protect the hull when moored alongside.

Fetch: The distance travelled by the wind when crossing open water: the height of the waves is proportional to the fetch and strength of the wind.

Fin keel: A steel keel bolted to the hull.

Fix: The position of a boat as plotted on the chart from position lines obtained by compass bearings, direction finder, echo sounder, etc.

Flake down: Rope laid down on deck in a figure aof eight pattern so that it will run out easily.

Flashing: A light used as an aid to navigation that flashes repeatedly at regular intervals.

Flood: The period when the tidal level is rising.

Fluke: The shovel-shaped part of an anchor that digs into the ground.

Flying out: A sail is flying out in a breeze when it has no tension in the sheets.

Focsle: The part of the accommodation below the foredeck and forward of the mast.

Fog: Visibility reduced to less than one thousand metres (approximately 0.5 nautical miles).

Foghorn: A horn with which fog signals are made.

Following sea: Seas that are moving in the same direction as the boat is heading.

Foot: The lower edge of a sail.

Fore-and-aft: Parallel line between the stem and the stern.

Foredeck: The part of the deck that is forward of the mast and coachroof.

Forefoot: The area below the water where the stem joins the keel.

Forehatch: A hatch forward, usually in the foredeck.

Forepeak: The most forward compartment in the bows of the boat.

Foresail: The headsail set on the forestay.

Forestay: The stay from high on the mast to the stemhead providing fore-and-aft support for the mast.

Foul: The opposite of clear; adverse (wind or tide); unsuitable.

Foul anchor: An anchor whose flukes are caught on an obstruction on the seabed or tangled with the cable.

Frap: Tie halyards to keep them off the mast to stop them rattling noisily in the wind when in harbour.

Freeboard: The vertical distance between the waterline and the top of the deck.

Free wind: The wind when it blows from a direction abaft the beam.

Front (air mass): Boundary between air masses at different temperatures.

Full and by: Close-hauled with all sails full and drawing; not pinching.

Full rudder: The maximum angle to which the rudder can be turned.

Furling: Rolling up or gathering and lashing a lowered sail using sail ties or shock-cord to prevent it from blowing about.

Gale: In the Beaufort scale, wind force 8, 34 to 40 knots. Severe gale, force 9, is 41 to 47 knots.

Galley: An area where food is prepared and cooked.

Gelcoat: The outer unreinforced layer of resin in a GRP hull.

Genoa: A large overlapping headsail set in light breezes.

Ghoster: A light full headsail set in light breezes.

Give-way vessel: The vessel whose duty it is to keep clear of another; she should take early and substantial action to avoid a collision.

Go about: To change from one tack to another by luffing and turning the bows through the wind.

Gong: A fog signal sounded in conjunction with a bell in a vessel over 100m in length when at anchor or aground.

Gooseneck: Fitting which attaches the boom to the mast.

Goosewing: To fly the headsail on the opposite side to the mainsail (using a spinnaker pole or whisker pole perhaps) when running.

Grab rail: Rails fitted above and below decks to grab at when the boat heels.

Ground: To run aground or touch the bottom either accidentally or deliberately.

Ground tackle: A general term for the anchors, cables and all the gear required when anchoring.

Groyne: *See* Breakwater.

GRP: Glass Reinforced Plastic.

Guardrail: Safety line fitted round the boat to prevent the crew from falling overboard.

Gunwale: The upper edge of the side of a boat.

Guy: A line attached to the end of a spar to keep it in position.

Gybe: To change from one tack to another by turning the stern through the wind.

Gybe-oh: The action of putting the helm across to gybe.

Hail: To shout loudly to crew in another boat.

Half hitch: A simple knot.

Halyard: A line or rope with which a sail, spar or flag is hoisted up a mast.

Hand-bearing compass: Portable magnetic compass with which visual bearings are taken.

Handrail: A wooden or metal rail on the coachroof or below deck which can be grabbed to steady a person.

Hanks: Fittings made of metal or nylon by which the luff of a staysail is held to a stay.

Hard: Hard ground where boats can be launched.

Hard and fast: Said of a boat that has run aground and is unable to get off immediately.

Harden in: To haul in the sheets to bring the sail closer to the centreline; the opposite of ease out.

Hatch: An opening in the deck that allows access to the accommodation.

Haul in: To pull in.

Hawse pipe: A hole in the bow of a vessel through which the anchor cable passes.

Haze: Visibility reduced to between 1,000 and 2,000 metres (0.5 to 1 nautical miles) by dry particles in suspension in the air.

Head: The bow or forward part of the boat. The upper corner of a triangular sail.

Head line: The mooring line or rope leading forward from the bows.

Head to wind: To point the stem of the boat into the wind.

Heading: The direction in which the boat's head is pointing, her course.

Headland: A fairly high and steep part of the land that projects into the sea.

Heads: The lavatory on a boat.

Headsail: Any sail set forward of the mast or of the foremast if there is more than one mast.

Headway: Movement through the water stem first.

Heat seal: To fuse the ends of the strands of a man-made fibre rope by heating.

Heaving line: A light line coiled ready for throwing; sometimes the end is weighted.

Heaving-to: A boat heaves-to when she goes about leaving the headsail sheeted on the original side so it is backed. Ideal manoeuvre for reefing in heavy weather.

Heel: To lean over to one side.

Height of tide: The vertical distance at any instant between sea level and chart datum.

Helmsman: The member of the crew who steers the boat.

Hitch: A type of knot.

Hoist: To raise an object vertically with a halyard.

Holding ground: The composition of the sea-bed that determines whether the anchor will hold well or not.

Hull: The body of a boat excluding masts, rigging and rudder.

Hull down: Said of a distant vessel when only the mast, sails and/or superstructure is visible above the horizon.

Hurricane: In the Beaufort scale, wind of force 12, 64 knots or above.

Hydrofoil: A boat with hydrofoils to lift the wetted surface of her hull clear of the water at speed.

Hydrography: The science of surveying the waters of the earth and adjacent land area, and publishing the results in charts, pilots, etc., for example Admiralty charts.

IALA: The International Association of Lighthouse Authorities which is responsible for the international buoyage system.

Impeller: Screw-like device which is rotated by water flowing past: used for measuring boat speed and distance travelled through the water.

In irons: Said of a boat that stops head to wind when going about.

Inflatable dinghy: A dinghy of synthetic rubber filled with air; can be deflated for stowage on board.

Inshore: Near to or towards or in the direction of the shore.

Isobar: On a synoptic chart, a line joining points of equal pressure.

Isophase: A light where the duration of light and darkness are equal.

Jackstay: A wire secured between two points.

Jam cleat (self jamming): A cleat with one horn shorter than the other designed so that a rope can be secured with a single turn.

Jib: Triangular headsail set on a stay forward of the mast.

Jury rig: A temporary but effective device that replaces lost or damaged gear.

Kedge anchor: A lightweight anchor used to move a boat or anchor temporarily in fine weather.

Keel: The main longitudinal beam on a boat between the stem and the stern.

Ketch: A two-masted boat where the after (mizzen) mast is smaller and is stepped forward of the rudder stock.

kHz (kilohertz): A measurement of frequency of radio waves equivalent to 1,000 cycles per second.

Kicking strap: Line or tackle to pull the boom down to keep it horizontal.

Kink: A sharp twist in a rope or wire rope; can be avoided by coiling the rope properly.

Knot: The unit of speed at sea; one nautical mile per hour; a series of loops in a rope or line.

Landfall: Land first sighted after a long voyage at sea.

Lanyard: A short length of line used to secure an object such as a knife.

Lash down: To secure firmly with a rope or line.

Lay: Strands twisted together to form a rope. To lay a mark is to sail direct to it without tacking.

Lead line: A line marked with knots at regular intervals and attached to a heavy weight; used to determine the depth of water.

Lee: The direction towards which the wind blows.

Leeboard: A board or strip of canvas along the open side of a berth to prevent the occupant from falling out.

Lee helm: The tendency of a boat to turn her bow to leeward.

Leech: The trailing edge of a triangular sail.

Lee-oh: The action of putting the helm across to go about.

Lee shore: A coastline towards which the onshore wind blows; the shore to leeward of a boat.

Leeward: Downwind, away from the wind, the direction towards which the wind blows.

Leeward boat: When two boats are on the same tack, the leeward boat is that which is to leeward of the other.

Leeway: The angular difference between the water track and the boat's heading. The effect of wind moving the boat bodily to leeward.

Lifeline: A wire or line attached at either end to a strong point and rigged along the deck to provide a handhold or to clip on a safety harness.

Line: Alternative name for small rope or for a rope used for mooring a boat.

Line of soundings: Numerous soundings taken at regular intervals.

List: A permanent lean to one side or the other.

List of lights: Official publication giving details of lights exhibited as aids to navigation.

Lively: Said of a boat that responds rapidly to the seas.

LOA: Length overall.

Loafer: A lightweight sail used when reaching or running in light winds.

Lock: A chamber with gates at each end in which the water level can be raised or lowered.

Locker: An enclosed stowage anywhere on board.

Locking turns: A reversed turn on a cleat to make a rope more secure; not advisable for halyards which may need to be cast off quickly.

Log: A device to measure a boat's speed or distance travelled through the water. *See* Deck Log.

Log reading: The reading of distance travelled through the water usually taken every hour from the log and recorded in the deck log.

Look-out: Visual watch; or the member of the crew responsible for keeping it.

Loom: The glow from a light below the horizon usually seen as a reflection on the clouds.

Lop: Short choppy seas.

Lose way: A boat loses way when she slows down and stops in the water.

Lubber line: The marker in the compass which is aligned with the fore-and-aft line of the boat against which the course can be read off on the compass card.

Luff: The leading edge of a fore-and-aft sail.

Lull: A temporary drop in wind speed.

Mainsail: The principal sail.

Mainsheet traveller: The athwartships slider to which the mainsheet tackle is made fast.

Make fast: To secure a line or rope to a cleat, mooring ring, bollard, etc.

Make heavy weather: Said of a yacht which rolls and pitches heavily, making slow and uncomfortable progress.

Make sail: To hoist the sails and get under way.

Make water: To leak but not by shipping water over the side.

Marina: Artificial boat harbour usually consisting of pontoons.

Mark: An object that marks a position.

Maroon: An explosive signal used to summon the crew when a lifeboat is called out.

Mast: The most important vertical spar without which no sail can be set.

Mast step: Fitting into which the mast heel fits.

Masthead light: A white light exhibited near the masthead by a power-driven vessel under way.

Masthead rig: A boat with the forestay attached to the masthead.

Mayday: The internationally recognised radio telephone distress signal.

Medico: When included in an urgency call (Pan Pan) on the radio telephone, medico indicates that medical advice is required.

MHWS (Mean High Water Springs): The average level of all high water at spring tides throughout the year: used as the datum level for heights of features on the chart.

Mist: Visibility reduced to between 1,000 and 2,000 metres (0.5 to 1 nautical miles) due to suspension of water particles in the air.

Mizzen mast: The smaller aftermast of a ketch or yawl.

Mole: A breakwater made of stone or concrete.

Monohull: A boat with a single hull.

Mooring: The ground tackle attached to a mooring buoy.

Mooring buoy: A non-navigational buoy to which a boat can moor.

Mooring ring: A ring on a mooring pile to which head and stern lines are secured.

Multihull: A boat with more than one hull such as a catamaran or trimaran.

Nautical almanac: Official publication giving positions of heavenly bodies and other information to enable a boat's position to be established.

Nautical mile: Unit of distance at sea based on the length of one minute of latitude.

Navel pipe: A pipe which passes through the deck to the anchor chain locker.

Navigation lights: Lights exhibited by all vessels between sunset and sunrise.

Neap tide: Tides where the range is least and the tidal streams run least strongly.

Near gale: Wind of Beaufort force 7, 28 to 33 knots.

Nominal range of a light: Nominal range of a light is dependent on its intensity: it is the luminous range when the meteorological visibility is 10 nautical miles.

No sail sector: An area either side of the wind, in which a boat cannot sail.

Not under command: A vessel unable to manoeuvre such as one whose rudder has been damaged.

Notices to mariners: Official notices issued weekly or at other times detailing corrections to charts and hydrographic publications.

Null: The bearing of a radio beacon at which the signal tends to disappear when the antenna of a direction finder is rotated.

Occulting light: A rhythmic light eclipsing at regular intervals so that the duration of light in each period is greater than the duration of darkness.

Offing: The part of the sea that is visible from the shore. To keep an offing is to keep a safe distance from the shore.

Oilskins: Waterproof clothing worn in foul weather.

On the bow: A direction about 45° from right ahead on either side of the boat.

On the quarter: a direction about 45° from right astern on either side of the boat.

Open: When two leading marks are not in line they are said to be open.

Osmosis: Water absorption through tiny pinholes in a GRP hull causing deterioration of the moulding.

Outhaul: A line with which the mainsail is hauled out along the boom.

Overcanvas: A boat carrying too much sail for the weather conditions.

Overfalls: Turbulent waters where there is a sudden change in depth or where two tidal streams meet.

Overtaking light: The white stern light; seen by an overtaking vessel when approaching from astern.

Painter: The line at the bow of a dinghy.

Pan pan: The internationally recognised radio telephone urgency signal which has priority over all the other calls except Mayday.

Parallel rules: Navigational instrument used in conjunction with the compass rose on a chart to transfer bearings and courses to plot a boat's position.

Pay off: The boat's head pays off when it turns to leeward away from the wind.

Pay out: To let out a line or rope gradually.

Period: Of a light, the time that it takes a rhythmic light to complete one sequence.

Pile: A stout timber or metal post driven vertically into a river or sea bed.

Pilot: An expert in local waters who assists vessels entering or leaving harbour. An official publication listing details of, for example, local coasts, dangers and harbours.

Pilot berth: A berth or bunk for use at sea.

Pinch: To sail too close to the wind so that the sails lose driving power.

Pipe cot: A spare berth on a pipe frame that hinges up when not in use.

Piston hanks: A hank on the luff of a staysail.

Pitch: The up and down motion of the bow and stern of a boat.

Pitchpole: A capsize in a following sea where the stern is lifted over the bow.

Play: To adjust a sheet continuously rather than cleating it. Movement of equipment such as the rudder in its mounting or housing.

Plot: To find a boat's position by laying off bearings on a chart.

Plough anchor: An anchor shaped like a ploughshare similar to a CQR anchor.

Point: The ability of a boat to sail close-hauled: the closer she sails the better she points. A division of 11° 15′ on the compass.

Poling out: Using a spar to push a foresail out when running.

Pontoon: A watertight tank, usually between piles, that rises and falls with the tide.

Pooped: A condition of a boat in which a following sea has broken over the stern into the cockpit.

Port hand: A direction on the port or left hand side of the boat.

Port side: The left hand side of a boat when looking towards the bow.

Position line: A line drawn on a chart by the navigator.

Pound: A boat pounds in heavy seas when the bows drop heavily after being lifted by a wave.

Prevailing wind: The wind direction that occurs most frequently at a place over a certain period.

Preventer: A line rigged from the end of the boom to the bow in heavy weather to prevent an accidental gybe.

Privileged vessel: The stand-on vessel in a collision situation: she should maintain her course and speed.

Pull: To row.

Pulpit: Stainless steel frame at the bow encircling the forestay to which the guardrails are attached.

Pushpit: Colloquial term for the stern pulpit.

Pyrotechnic: Any type of rocket or flare used for signalling.

Quarter: The side of the hull between amidships and astern.

Quarter berth: A berth that extends under the deck between the cockpit and the hull.

Race: A strong tidal stream.

Radar reflector: A device hoisted or fitted up the mast to enhance the reflection of radar energy.

Radio direction finder: A radio receiver with a directional aerial that enables the navigator to find the direction from which a radio signal arrives.

Raft of boats: Two or more boats tied up alongside each other.

Range of tide: The difference between sea level at high water and sea level at the preceding or following low water.

Rate: The speed of a tidal stream or current given in knots and tenths of a knot.

RDF: Radio Direction Finder.

Reach: A boat is on a reach when she is neither close-hauled or running. It is her fastest point of sail.

Ready about: The helmsman's shout that he intends to go about shortly.

Reciprocal course: The course (or bearing) that differs by 180°.

Reed: A weak high-pitched fog signal.

Reef: To reduce the area of sail, particularly the mainsail.

Reef points: Short light lines sewn into the sail parallel with the boom that are tied under the foot (or under the boom itself) when the sail is reefed in high winds.

Reefing pendants: A strong line with which the luff and leech are pulled down to the boom when a sail is reefed.

Relative bearing: The direction of an object relative to the fore-and-aft line of a boat measured in degrees from right ahead.

Relative wind: *See* Apparent Wind.

Restricted visibility: Visibility restricted by rain, drizzle, fog, etc., during which vessels are required to proceed at a safe speed and to navigate with extreme caution.

Rhumb line: A line on the surface of the earth that cuts all meridians at the same angle. On a standard (mercator) chart the rhumb line appears as a straight line.

Ride: To lie at anchor free to swing to the wind and tidal stream.

Ridge: On a synoptic chart, a narrow area of relatively high pressure between two low pressure areas.

Riding light: Alternative term for anchor light.

Riding turn: On a winch the situation where an earlier turn rides over a later turn and jams.

Rigging: All ropes, lines, wires and gear used to support the masts and to control the spars and sails.

Right of way: Term used for the vessel which does not give way.

Risk of collision: A possibility that a collision may occur; usually established by taking a compass bearing of an approaching vessel.

Roads: An anchorage where the holding ground is known to be good and there is some protection from the wind and sea.

Roll: The periodic rotating movement of a boat that leans alternately to port and starboard.

Roller reef: A method of reefing where the sail area is reduced by rolling part of the sail around the boom.

Rolling hitch: A knot used to attach a small line to a larger line or spar.

Rotator: A metal spinner with vanes which rotates when a boat moves through the water actuating the log on board to which it is attached by a log line.

Round: To sail around a mark.

Round turn: A complete turn of a rope or line around an object. The rope completely encircles the object.

Round up: To head up into the wind.

Roving fender: A spare fender held ready by a crew member in case of emergencies.

Rowlock: A space in the gunwhale in which the oar is placed.

Rubbing Strake: A projecting strake round the top of a hull to protect the hull when lying alongside.

Rudder: A control surface in the water at or near the stern, used for altering course.

Run: The point of sailing where a boat sails in the same direction as the wind is blowing with her sheets eased right out.

Run down: To collide with another boat.

Runner: A backstay that supports the mast from aft and can be slacked off.

Running fix: A navigational fix when only a single landmark is available. Two bearings are taken and plotted at different times making allowance for distance travelled.

Running rigging: All rigging that moves and is not part of the standing rigging.

Sacrificial anode: A zinc plate fastened to the hull to prevent corrosion of metal fittings on the hull.

Sail locker: Place where sails are stowed.

Sail ties: Light lines used to lash a lowered sail to the boom or guardrails to prevent it blowing about.

Sailing directions: Also called Pilots. Official publications covering specific areas containing navigational information concerning, for example, coasts, harbours and tides.

Sailing free: Not close-hauled; sailing with sheets eased out.

Saloon: The main cabin.

Salvage: The act of saving a vessel from danger at sea.

Samson post: Strong fitting bolted firmly to the deck around which anchor cables, mooring lines or tow ropes are made fast.

SAR: Search and Rescue.

Scend: Vertical movement of waves or swell against, for example, a harbour wall.

Scope: The ratio of the length of anchor cable let out to the depth of water.

Scupper: Drain hole in the toe-rail.

Sea anchor: A device, such as a conical canvas bag open at both ends, streamed from bow or stern to hold a boat bow or stern on to the wind or sea.

Sea breeze: A daytime wind blowing across a coastline from the sea caused by the rising air from land heated by the sun.

Sealegs: The ability to keep one's feet in spite of the motion of the boat.

Seacock: A stop-cock next to the hull to prevent accidental entry of water.

Searoom: An area in which a vessel can navigate without difficulty or danger of hitting an obstruction.

Seaway: A stretch of water where there are waves.

Securite: An internationally recognised safety signal used on the radio telephone preceding an important navigational or meteorological warning.

Seize: To bind two ropes together.

Serve: To cover and protect a splice on a rope by binding with small line or twine.

Set (sails): To hoist a sail.

Set (tidal stream): The direction to which a tidal stream or current flows.

Set sail: To start out on a voyage.

Shackle: A metal link for connecting ropes, wires or chains to sails, anchors, etc. To shackle on is to connect using a shackle.

Shape: A ball, cone or diamond shaped object, normally black, hoisted by day in a vessel to indicate a special state or occupation.

Sheave: A wheel over which a rope or wire runs.

Sheer off: To turn away from another vessel or object in the water.

Sheet: Rope or line fastened to the clew of a sail or the end of the boom supporting it. Named after the sail to which it is attached.

Sheet bend: A knot used to join two ropes of different size together.

Sheet in: To pull in on a sheet till it is taut and the sail drawing.

Shelving: A gradual slope in the seabed.

Shipping forecast: Weather forecast broadcast four times each day by the British Broadcasting Corporation for the benefit of those at sea.

Shipping lane: A busy track across the sea or ocean.

Shipshape: Neat and efficient.

Shoal: An area offshore where the water is so shallow that a ship might run aground. To shoal is to become shallow.

Shock cord: Elastic rubber bands enclosed in a sheath of fibres, very useful for lashing.

Shorten in: Decrease the amount of anchor cable let out.

Shorten sail: To reduce the amount of sail set either by reefing or changing to make a smaller sail.

Shrouds: Parts of the standing rigging that support the mast laterally.

Sidedeck: The deck alongside the coachroof.

Sidelight: The red and green lights exhibited either side of the bows by vessels under way and making way through the water.

Sill: A wall which acts as a dam, to keep water in a marina.

Siren: The fog signal made by vessels over 12 metres in length when under way.

Skeg: A false keel fitted near the stern which supports the leading edge of the rudder.

Skylight: A framework fitted on the deck of a boat with glazed windows to illuminate the cabin and provide ventilation.

Slab reef: A method of reefing a boomed sail where the sail is flaked down on top of the boom.

Slack off: To ease or pay out a line.

Slack water: In tidal waters, the period of time when the tidal stream is non-existent or negligible.

Slam: The underpart of the forward part of the hull hitting the water when pitching in heavy seas.

Slide: A metal or plastic fitting on the luff or foot of a sail running in a track on the mast or boom.

Sliding hatch: A sliding hatch fitted over the entrance to the cabin.

Slip: To let go quickly.

Sliplines: Mooring ropes or lines doubled back so that they can be let go easily from on board.

Slipway: An inclined ramp leading into the sea.

Snap hook: A hook that springs shut when released.

Snap shackle: A shackle that is held closed by a spring-loaded plunger.

Snarl up: Lines or ropes that are twisted or entangled.

Snatch: Jerk caused by too short an anchor cable in a seaway. To take a turn quickly around a cleat, bollard or samson post.

Snug down: To prepare for heavy weather by securing all loose gear.

Soldier's wind: A wind that enables a sailing boat to sail to her destination and return without beating.

Sole: The floor of a cabin or cockpit.

SOS: International distress signal made by light, sound or radio.

Sound: To measure the depth of water.

Sounding: The depth of water below chart datum.

Sou'wester: A waterproof oilskin hat with a broad brim.

Spar: General term for all poles used on board such as mast, boom and yard.

Speed made good: The speed made good over the ground; that is, the boat speed corrected for tidal stream and leeway.

Spill wind: To ease the sheets so that the sail is only partly filled by the wind, the rest being spilt.

Spindrift: Fine spray off wave crests caused by strong winds.

Spinnaker: A large symmetrical balloon shaped sail used when running or reaching.

Spinnaker pole: A spar which is used to hold the spinnaker out.

Spit: A projecting shoal or strip of land connected to the shore.

Splice: A permanent joint made between two ropes.

Split ring: A ring like a key ring that can be fed into an eye to prevent accidental withdrawal.

Spray hood: A folding canvas cover over the entrance to the cabin.

Spreaders: Metal struts fitted either side of the mast to spread the shrouds out sideways.

Spring tide: The tides at which the range is greatest: the height of high water is greater and that for low water is less than those for neap tides.

Springs: Moorings lines fastened to prevent a boat moving forwards or backwards relative to the quay or other boats alongside.

Squall: A sudden increase of wind speed often associated with a line of low dark clouds representing an advancing cold front.

Stanchions: Metal posts supporting the guardrails.

Standby to gybe: A warning, given by the helmsman, that he is about to gybe.

Stand in: To head towards land.

Stand off: To head away from the shore.

Standing rigging: Wire rope or solid rods that support masts and fixed spars but do not control the sails.

Starboard side: The right side when looking forward towards the bow.

Stay: Part of the standing rigging which provides support fore and aft.

Staysail: A sail set on a stay.

Steady: Order to the helmsman to keep the boat on her present course.

Steaming light: Alternative term for masthead light.

Steep-to: A sharply sloping seabed.

Steerage way: A boat has steerage way when she is moving fast enough to answer to the helm; that is, to respond to deflections of the rudder.

Steering compass: The compass permanently mounted adjacent to the helmsman which he uses as a reference to keep the boat on a given course.

Stem: The forewardmost part of the hull.

Stemhead: The top of the stem.

Stemhead fitting: A fitting on the stemhead, often an anchor roller.

Stern: The afterpart of the boat.

Stern gland: Packing around the propeller shaft where it passes through the hull.

Stern light: A white light exhibited from the stern.

Stern line: The mooring line going aft from the stern.

Sternsheets: The aftermost part of an open boat.

Stiff: A boat that does not heel easily; opposite to tender.

Stopper knot: A knot made in the end of a rope to prevent it running out through a block or fairlead.

Storm: Wind of Beaufort force 10, 48 to 55 knots; or a violent storm force 11, 56 to 63 knots.

Storm jib: Small heavy jib set in strong winds.

Stormbound: Confined to a port or anchorage by heavy weather.

Stove in: A hull that has been broken inwards.

Stow: Put away in a proper place. Stowed for sea implies that all gear and loose equipment has, in addition, been lashed down.

Strand: To run a vessel aground intentionally or accidentally.

Strop: A loop of wire rope fitted round a spar. A wire rope used to add length to the luff of a headsail.

Strum box: A strainer fitted around the suction end of a bilge pump hose to prevent the pump being choked by debris.

Strut: A small projecting rod.

Suit: A complete set of sails.

Surge: To ease a rope out round a winch or bollard.

Swashway: A narrow channel between shoals.

Sweat up: To tauten a rope as much as possible.

Sweep: A long oar.

Swig: To haul a line tight when it is under load, by pulling it out at right angles and quickly taking in the slack.

Swing: To rotate sideways on a mooring in response to a change in direction of the tidal stream or wind.

Swinging room: The area encompassed by a swing that excludes any risk of collision or of grounding.

Synopsis: A brief statement outlining the weather situation at a particular time.

Synoptic chart: A weather chart covering a large area on which is plotted information giving an overall view of the weather at a particular moment.

Tack: To go about from one course to another with the bow passing through the eye of the wind. A sailing boat is on a tack if she is neither gybing nor tacking; the lower forward corner of a sail.

Tackle: A combination of rope and blocks designed to increase the pulling or hoisting power of a line.

Take in: Lower a sail.

Take the helm: Steer the boat.

Take way off: To reduce the speed of the boat.

Telltales: Lengths of wool or ribbon attached to the sails or shrouds to indicate the airflow or apparent direction of the wind.

Tender: A boat that heels easily is said to be tender; the opposite of stiff.

Thwart: The athwartships seat in a small boat or dinghy.

Tidal stream: The horizontal movement of water caused by the tides.

Tidal stream atlas: An official publication showing the direction and rate of the tidal streams for a particular area.

Tide: The vertical rise and fall of the waters in the oceans in response to the gravitational forces of the sun and moon.

Tide tables: Official annual publication which gives the times and heights of high and low water for standard ports and the differences for secondary ports.

Tideway: The part of a channel where the tidal stream runs most strongly.

Tiller: A lever attached to the rudder head by which the helmsman deflects the rudder.

Time (4 figure notation): Time is given in a four figure notation based on the 24-hour clock.

Toe-rail: A low strip of wood or light alloy that runs round the edge of a deck.

Toggle: A small piece of wood inserted in an eye to make a quick connection.

Topping lift: A line from the base of the mast passing around a sheave at the top thence to the end of the boom to take the weight of the boom when lowering the sail.

Topsides: The part of the boat which lies above the waterline when she is not heeled.

Track: The path between two positions: ground track is that over the ground; water track is that through the water.

Traffic separation scheme: In areas of heavy traffic, a system of one-way lanes. Special regulations apply to shipping in these zones.

Transceiver: A radio transmitter and receiver.

Transducer: A component that converts electric signals into sound waves and vice versa.

Transferred position line: A position line for one time, transferred, with due allowance for the vessel's ground track, to cross with another position line at a later time.

Transit: Two fixed objects are in transit when they are in line.

Transom: The flat transverse structure across the stern of a hull.

Traveller: The sliding car on a track, for example on the main sheet track or adjustable headsail sheet block.

Trawler: A fishing vessel that fishes using nets trawled along the sea-bed.

Trick: Spell on duty, especially at the helm.

Tri-colour light: A single light at the top of the mast of sailing boats under 20 metres long that can be used in place of the navigation lights.

Trim: To adjust the sails by easing or hardening in the sheets to obtain maximum driving force.

Trip-line: A line attached to the crown of an anchor to enable it to be pulled out backwards if it gets caught fast by an object on the sea-bed.

Trot: Mooring buoys laid in a line.

Truck: The very top of the mast.

Trysail: A small heavy sail set on the mast in stormy weather in place of the mainsail.

Tune: To improve the performance of a sailing boat or engine.

Twilight: Period before sunrise and after sunset when it is not yet dark.

Twine: Small line used for sewing and whipping.

Unbend: To unshackle sheets and halyards and remove a sail ready to stow.

Underway: A vessel is underway if it is not at anchor, made fast to the shore or aground.

Unshackle: To unfasten.

Unship: To remove an object from its working position.

Up and down: Said of an anchor cable when it is vertical.

Uphaul: A line which is used to raise a spar vertically.

Upstream: The direction from which the river flows.

Upwind: The direction from which the wind is blowing.

Vang: A tackle or strap fitted between the boom and the toe-rail to keep the boom horizontal.

Variation: The angle between the true and the magnetic meridian for any geographical position.

Veer: Of a cable or line, to pay out gradually. Of the wind, to change direction clockwise.

Ventilator (vent): A fitting which allows fresh air to enter the boat.

VHF: Very High Frequency; usually taken as meaning the VHF radio telephone.

Visibility: The greatest distance at which an object can be seen against its background.

Wake: Disturbed water left by a moving boat. The direction of the wake compared with the fore-and-aft line of the boat is often used as a rough measure of leeway.

Warp: Heavy lines used for mooring, kedging or towing, and to move a boat by hauling on warps secured to a bollard or buoy.

Wash: The turbulent water left astern by a moving boat.

Washboards: Removable planks fitted in the cabin entrance to prevent water getting in.

Watch: One of the periods into which 24 hours is divided on board.

Waterline: The line along the hull at the surface of the water in which she floats.

Wear: To change tacks by gybing.

Weather a mark: To succeed in passing to windward of a mark.

Weather helm: The tendency of a boat to turn her bow to windward making it necessary to hold the tiller to the weather side.

Weep: To leak slowly.

Weigh anchor: To raise the anchor.

Well: A sump in the bilges. A small locker for the anchor.

Wheel: The steering wheel that moves the rudder.

Whipping: Twine bound round the ends of a rope to keep it from fraying.

Whisker pole: Light spar to hold out the clew of a headsail when running, particularly when goosewinged.

Whistle: An appliance to make sound signals in restricted visibility and when manoeuvring.

White horses: Breaking waves with foamy crest. Not surf breaking on the shore.

Winch: A fitting designed to assist the crew hauling on a rope or line.

Winch handle: A removable handle used for operating a winch.

Windage: All parts of a boat that contribute to total air drag.

Windlass: The winch used for weighing the anchor.

Windward: The direction from which the wind blows.

Withies: Branches used in small rivers to mark the edges of the channel.

Yankee jib: A large jib set forward of the staysail in light winds.

Yard: A long spar on which a square sail is set.

Yawing: Swinging from side to side of the course set, or at anchor.

Yawl: A two-masted boat where the mizzen mast is aft of the rudder stock.

QUESTIONS

23.1   Fill in the following on the diagram:
   a. coachroof
   b. cockpit
   c. anchor locker
   d. side deck
   e. foredeck

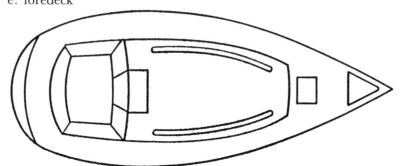

23.2   Draw a sketch to show parts of the mainsail.

23.3   Explain the following terms:
   a. Headway
   b. Broach
   c. Sea-room
   d. Tender
   e. Beam

23.4   What is a *Notice to Mariners*?

23.5   What is the purpose of a sacrificial anode?

Chapter Twenty-four

Test Paper B: General

B1. Using the tidal stream atlas Fig 8.1 and Extract 1, what is the tidal stream off Anvil Point at 1300 BST on 22nd August?

B2. What is the depth of water over a 1.5 metre sounding in Dover at 1025 BST on 18th May?

B3. In the following situations a risk of collision exists. In each case state the action to be taken by the skipper of boat 'B'.

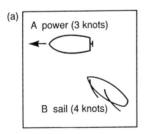
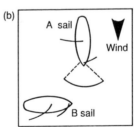
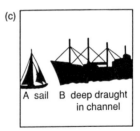

B4. You are heading south when, dead ahead, you sight a buoy with the following topmark: two cones base to base.

   a. What type of buoy is indicated?
   b. Which way should you alter course?
   c. What would be the characteristics of the light?

B5. Identify the most suitable knot for the listed tasks:
   a. Attaching a sheet to the clew of a headsail.
   b. Fastening a rope to the eye of an eyesplice.
   c. Tying a mooring line to a ring bolt.
   d. A stopper knot in a rope's end.
   e. Joining two ropes of unequal diameters.

B6. You are the owner of a 10 metre sailing boat. State which lights you would show at night in the following circumstances:
   a. Under engine entering harbour
   b. Under sail assisted by the engine running at half power
   c. Under sail running on the starboard tack
   d. At anchor in a fairway

B7. Which type of rope should be used for the following applications?
   a. Main halyard
   b. Genoa sheet
   c. Safety line attached to a lifebelt
   d. Anchor cable

B8. You are sailing on the starboard tack up an estuary in fog. What fog signal must you make and at what intervals?

B9. List 8 international distress signals.

B10. Your sailing yacht *Dabbler* strikes an underwater object and is in danger of sinking. You have a crew consisting of one man, two women, a 2-year-old infant and yourself as skipper. You see Anvil Point to the north about 2 miles distant. What is the distress call and message that you would transmit on the VHF radio?

B11. What Beaufort wind force would give the following sea conditions?
   Moderate waves taking a more pronounced long form, many white horses, chance of some spray.

B12. Explain the following terms used in a Shipping Forecast:
   a. Moving steadily
   b. Poor visibility
   c. Expected soon

B13. What is the magnetic bearing for each of the following true bearings?
   a. 156°(T) Variation 3°E
   b. 357°(T) Variation 4°W
   c. 003°(T) Variation 5°E

B14. On a Stanfords chart what colour is used to indicate a sandbank that dries out at chart datum?

B15. What will the magnetic variation be in the vicinity of Poole Fairway buoy (50° 39′N 1° 55′W) in 1998?

Answers to Questions

1.1 Chart 15 is a **much larger scale** than chart 12 so will include more detail.

1.2 Poole Harbour and approaches.

1.3a. **The latitude scale.**
 b. **The longitude scale.**

1.4 By **using the latitude and longitude scales** as a reference.

1.5 One nautical mile per hour.

CHAPTER TWO

2.1 During projection distortion occurs on the chart. On a mercator projection chart the distance scale increases as latitude increases, therefore **one minute of latitude is equivalent to one nautical mile** *only* **in the area of the boat's position.**

2.2 Meridians of longitude appear as **straight lines** in a north-south direction. **Parallels of latitude** appear as **straight parallel lines** in an east-west direction (at right angles to meridians of longitude). Any **Rhumb Line course crosses all meridians and parallels of latitude at the same angle.**

2.3 There is **too much distortion.**

2.4 The **Greenwich meridian** which passes through London.

2.5 50° 38′.5.

CHAPTER THREE

3.1 Anvil Point lighthouse.

3.2a. **0.1M.**
 b. **0.05M.**

3.3a. **023°T.**
   b. **4.7M.**
   c. **1h 03m.**

3.4 This should be close to **East Hook buoy.**

3.5 **50° 36'.0N 1° 55'.0W.**

CHAPTER FOUR

4.1 4° 02'W.

4.2a. 224°M, 143°M, 009°M.
   b. **352°T, 185°T, 012°T.**

4.3a. 001°C, 004°C, 158°C.
   b. **231°M, 066°M, 289°M.**

4.4 The deviation for *all three* bearings is 4°E which is the figure shown on the deviation table corresponding to the boat's heading of 060°C.
   a. **Tower 089°T; Church 165°T; Monument 328°T.**
   b. **2°W.**

4.5 Well away from anything likely to cause deviation (electrical equipment, magnets, ferrous metal); **accurately aligned with the fore-and-aft line of the boat;** where it can **easily be seen by the helmsman;** and where **it will not suffer damage.**

CHAPTER FIVE

5.1 Symbols and Abbreviations used on Admiralty Charts (chart booklet 5011).

5.2a. Rock awash at the level of chart datum; Visitor's mooring; Marina.
   b. **Foul ground; Anchorage; Water Tower (52).**
   c. **Fine sand.**

5.3 Just under 1m.

5.4 Tide race on the ebb.

5.5 45m

CHAPTER SIX

6.1 The lowest level to which the tide is expected to fall due to astronomical conditions.

6.2 Yes: due to abnormal meteorological conditions such as **high**

barometric pressure or strong offshore winds blowing for a period of several days.

6.3a. The depth of water below Chart Datum.
   b. In metres and decimeters.

6.4   Mean High Water Springs (MHWS) which is the mean of the spring tide high waters throughout the year.

6.5   At spring tides.

CHAPTER SEVEN

7.1   From Admiralty Tide Tables, Yachtsmen's Almanacs and local tide tables.

7.2   3.8m.

7.3   4.2m.

	HW		LW	Range
Dover GMT	1517	6.1	1.1	5.0 (0.3 from Sps)
	+ 0100			
BST	1617			

Interval: HW + 3h 03m

7.4   1228 BST.

	HW		LW	Range
Dover GMT	1348	5.9	1.5	4.4 (0.5 from Sps)
Differences	+ 0020	– 1.6	– 0.6	
Ramsgate GMT	1408	4.3	0.9	
	+ 0100			
BST	1508			

Interval: HW – 2h 40m

7.5   1.3m.

	HW	LW		Range
Portsmouth GMT	4.0	0738	1.3	1.7 (Nps)
Differences	– 1.4	– 0027	– 0.2	
Yarmouth GMT	2.6	0711	1.1	
		+ 0100		
BST		0811		

Interval: LW + 2h 04m

CHAPTER EIGHT

8.1   180°T 1.1 knots.

8.2   HW + 6 to HW − 1. Six hours after high water to one hour before high water.

8.3   Tabulated values are mean values. **Considerable variation may occur at spring tides.**

8.4   Often the tidal streams in bays are slacker or on some occasions there is a contrary stream. In this case the boats are **lying head to wind indicating that there is little or no tidal stream.**

8.5   Sail close to the buoy and look at the tidal stream around it.

CHAPTER NINE

9.1a.   i. **A white tower.** ii. **A white light flashing every 10 seconds.**
    b.   **17M.** In the light characteristics the figure 24M is the nominal range of the light (the range at which the light would be visible when the meteorological visibility is 10 miles). This does not take into account the curvature of the earth. There are tables in Yachtsmen's Almanacs which give the range of a light knowing the height of the light and the height of the observer's eye. For the height of the light, allowance also has to be made for the state of the tide. For a height of eye of 2m and a height of light of 45m, the range of a light would be 17M.
    c.   **A horn sounding 3 blasts every 30 seconds.**

9.2   No: it is obscured. **The castle on Durlston Head, Handfast Point.**

9.3   There is no major reason not to use the inshore passage at night as it is adequately lit. Check that the characteristics of the white light are those of Poole Fairway buoy, then plot the position on the chart. Proceed on a northerly course until the red light bears 310°M but keep a good lookout for the unlit East Hook buoy. Alter course until the East Looe buoy (quick flashing red) is passed to port. Alter course to 255°T (260°M) heading for the main channel watching out for the unlit north cardinal beacon which is left to port. Keep a careful check on the depth using the echo-sounder. The depth will also indicate when the main channel has been reached.

9.4   The **ferry is about to start. Navigate with caution.** In practice it would be courteous to give way to the ferry.

9.5a.   Maintain a course to keep Anvil Point light visible clear of Durlston Head. When the main lights in the town of Swanage can be seen clear of Peveril Point, identify the 2 fixed red vertical lights on Swanage pier and use them as a clearing bearing (which should not be greater than 277°M) to proceed towards the anchorage off Swanage.

    b. **Two fixed red vertical lights.**

CHAPTER TEN

10.1 Course 014°T, Water track 014°T, Distance run 1.9M
    a. **50°37′.3N 1°53′.7W**
    b. **50°37′.6N 1°53′.2W**
    c. **021°T**
    d. **4.4k**

10.2 Course 350°T, Water track 350°T, Distance run 2.5M
       Course 090°T, Water track 090°T, Distance run 2.5M
       EP 50°39′.7N 1°44′.0W

10.3 Course 001°T, Distance run 1.7M
       344°T 1.4k

10.4 Course 051°M, 046°T, Water track 056°T
       Course 320°M, 315°T, Water track 305°T
       Tidal streams: (A) 049° 1.0k (B) 354° 0.5k
       EP (1250) 50°38′.4N 1°49′.1W
       EP (1320) 50°39′.8N 1°51′.7W

10.5 Course (1600–1700) 283°M, 278°T, Water track 273°T, Distance run 4.1M
       Course (1700–1703) 231°M, 226°T, Water track 226°T, Distance run 0.2M
       Course (1703–1749) 231°M, 226°T, Water track 226°T, Distance run 2.7M
       EP (1700) 50°42′.6N 1°52′.0W
       EP (1749) 50°40′.7N 1°55′.3W
       East Hook buoy

CHAPTER ELEVEN

11.1a. **50°35′.4N 1°57′.5W.**
    b. **A sounding would have shown that the boat was over the 10m depth contour.** With only 2 bearings the angle of cut should be around 90°: the right hand edge of Durlston Head would have given a better cut.
    c. The most probable cause is **a tidal stream stronger than anticipated.**

11.2a. The true bearing of the transit of the beacons (from the chart) is 354°T, hence the magnetic bearing is 359°M. The deviation is therefore **4°E.**

b. **No:** it is only valid for the boat's present heading of 263°C and will alter as the heading changes.

c. **No:** transit bears 354°T.

d. The hand-bearing compass is only free from deviation if it is used **well clear of all magnetic influences.**

11.3 Anvil Point light 279°T. Course 009°T.
Water track 015°T.
Handfast Point 348 °T. Distance run 1.9M
Tidal stream 049°T 1.0k.

a. **50°37'.5N 1°54'.9W.**

b. The accuracy of a transferred position line (running fix) depends on the **correct assessment of the tidal stream and leeway together with an accurate course and distance run** from the log.

c. **168°T Handfast Point 1.1M.**

11.4

Bournemouth pier	281°T
Boscombe pier	047°T
Hotel	000°T
Yellow buoy	262°T

a. **50°42'.6N 1°51'.2W.**

b. The three bearings of the shore landmarks intersect at the same point: the **buoy is not exactly in the position shown on the chart.**

11.5a. **No:** the depth corrected to charted depth is 10.5m which only indicates that boat is in the vicinity of the 10m depth contour. Approximate position 50° 42' 6N 1° 46'.0W.

b. The boat is heading for Beerpan Rocks (at a distance of 0.6M) with insufficient depth of water to clear them. She **would alter course to 114° M** until the CG Lookout and the beacon on the end of the groyne are in transit.

CHAPTER TWELVE

12.1 Water track 070°T. Course 080°T, **085°M.** Speed made good 4.1k.

12.2 Distance to go about 5M. Tidal stream 156°T 0.6k. Water track 221°T. Course 226°T, 231°T, **231°M.** Speed made good 4.3k. Time taken 1h 08m. **ETA 1858.**

12.3 Distance to go 3.9M. Tidal streams: (A) HW–3: 053°T 1.0k; (B) HW–2: 029°T 0.2k. Water track 288°T. Course 278°T, **283°M.** Distance made good 4.6M, speed made good 2.3k. Time taken 1h 42m. **ETA 1732.**

12.4   Tidal stream: 1150–1250, HW–5: 049°T 1.0k; 1250–1350, HW–4: 354°T 0.5k. Speed made good 4.0k. (It is not necessary to plot a tidal vector for the first part as the tidal stream is along track: speed made good = speed + tidal stream = 3.0 + 1.0 = 4.0.) Time taken 1h. Water track 050°T. Course 040°T, **045°M**. The boat tacks in position 50°38′.0N 1°50′.8W. Distance to go to buoy 2.7M. Time taken 51m. Water track 282°T, Course 292°T, **297°M**. Speed made good 3.2k. **ETA 1341.**

12.5   Distance to go about 3.4M. Tidal stream 344°T 1.4k (Plot 30 minute vector: 344°T 0.7M.) Water track 023°T. Course 023°T, **028°M**. Distance made good 3.6M; speed made good 7.2k. Time taken 29 minutes. **ETA 0929.**

CHAPTER THIRTEEN

13.1a.   **Local weather centre.**
   b.   **By listening to the shipping forecast.**

13.2   **Listen to the Coast Radio station** at Niton at 0833 (GMT) or **contact the Coastguard** (Channel 16 then Channel 67) and request a weather report.

13.3   The prolonged blast indicates a power-driven vessel underway. The immediate action is to **slow down and keep well over to the starboard side of the channel** sounding the appropriate fog signal. The subsequent action may be to **alter course for Studland Bay and acnhor until the visibility improves.**

13.4   As the wind has been blowing in the same direction for two days, a wave pattern will have been built up and may not disappear immediately with the wind shift. The new wind direction may cause a new wave pattern superimposed on the other. The coastline down to Anvil point will give some protection but there are tide races on the ebb tide around the headlands which cause steep seas that will be unpleasant if not dangerous.
   a.   **The motor boat would roll and pitch heavily in the seas with spray on deck. She would need to slow down in the rough seas off the headlands.**
   b.   **The fin-keeled sailing boat would be heeled well over even if reefed with plenty of spray on deck and pitching heavily. Progress will be slow.**
   c.   **The bilge-keel sailing boat will make little or no progress in the heavy seas. She would pitch and roll uncomfortably and the waves may frequently break over the deck.**

13.5a.   **1000m to 2M.**
   b.   **Between 35k and 45k.**

c. **Beaufort Force 7: 28k-33k.**
d. **Beaufort Force 4: 11k-16k.**
e. **From 12 to 24 hours hence.**

CHAPTER SIXTEEN

16.1 *Refer to plot (see front endpaper).*
16.2 Plate 4 **Christchurch harbour entrance (50°43'.4N 1°43'.9W)**
Plate 5 **Groyne of Hengistbury Head (50°42'.5N 1°45'.0W)**
Plate 6 **CG Lookout – Hengistbury Head (50°42'.6N 1° 45'.5W)**
Plate 7 **Christchurch Priory (50°42'.6N 1°46'.1W)**
Plate 8 **Water Tower (conspic) (50°42'.6N 1°48'.1W)**
Plate 9 **Bournemouth – St Peter's church (50°42'.5N 1°52'.3W)**
Plate 10 **Bournemouth – Hotel (conspic) (50°42'.2N 1°53'.4W)**
Plate 11 **Poole Fairway – Handfast Point (50°39'.1N 1°54'.7W)**
Plate 12 **Handfast Point – Durlston Head (50°38'.8N 1°55'.2W)**
Plate 13 **Handfast Point (50°38'.5N 1°55'.0W)**
Plate 14 **Peveril Ledge – Durlston Head (50°36'.5N 1°55'.9W)**
Plate 15 **Peveril Point (50°36'.5N 1°56'.5W)**
Plate 16 **Swanage pier (50°36'.5N 1°56'.7W)**
Plate 17 **Swanage town (50°36'.6N 1°57'.1W)**

16.3 Anvil Point lighthouse. The photograph was taken on a bearing of 080°T from the lighthouse. The **lighthouse becomes obscurred** from a more northerly position.

CHAPTER SEVENTEEN

17.1 The deck log might be entered as follows:

FROM: *Swanage*   TO: *Wareham*   DATE: *10th July*

TIME:		LOG	COURSE (°M)	WIND	BARO
1630	Weighed anchor in Swanage Bay. Set course 044°M under power	12.5	044	E4	1026
1640	Hoisted main and working jib. Stopped engine	13.1	044		
1651	Ballard Point abeam	13.8	044		

TIME		LOG	COURSE (°M)	WIND	BARO
1700		14.4	044	E4	1026
1703	Handfast Point abeam. Altered course 344°M for Swash channel	14.5	344		
1708	Poole Fairway buoy abeam	14.9	344		
1714	Entered Swash channel between Bar buoy and No 2 buoy. Followed channel	15.3	344		
1733	No 16 buoy to port. Started engine and lowered sails	16.5	Var		
1735	Passed chain ferry				
1744	Passed Bell buoy opposite Brownsea Castle. Followed Middle Ship channel	17.2	Var		
1750	Shipping forecast: Portland, Wight SE 5–6 Moderate to good				
1800		18.1	Var	ESE3	1027
1807	Stakes buoy abeam. Followed Wareham channel	18.5	Var		
1831	Passed Dorset Yacht Co jetty	19.9	Var		
1900	Gigger's Isle to port	21.6	Var	SE2	1027
1926	Passed Ridge Wharf yacht centre	23.1	Var		
1950	Secured to visitor's berth on Wareham Quay. Engine stopped	24.5	Var		

17.2   Plate 19 **Ballard Point (50°37'.5N 1°55'.8W)**
Plate 20 **Haven Hotel (50°40'.8N 1°56'.8W)**
Plate 21 **East Looe channel (50°41'.0N 1°56'.1W)**
Plate 22 **Chain ferry (50°40'.8N 1°56'.8W)**
Plate 23 **Bell buoy (50°41'.3N 1°56'.8W)**
Plate 24 **Ro-Ro terminal (50°42'.4N 1°59'.0W)**
Plate 25 **No. 67 buoy (50°42'.2N 1°59'.6W)**
Plate 26 **No. 76 buoy (50°42'.7N 2°02'.1W)**

17.3   Plate 27 **Poole bridge (50°42'.7N 1°59'.3W)**

TEST PAPER A

Refer to plot for answers A1 to A8 (see pages 198–9).

A1.   50°35'.5N 1°44'.6W.

Mag Course	Var	True Course	Leeway	Water Track	
230	5°W	225	5°	220	stbd tack
320	5°W	315	5°	320	port tack

A.2   Plot the ground track on the port tack for a period of 2 hours using tidal diamond A. To reach Poole Fairway buoy it will be necessary to tack at around 1300. From the buoy plot the ground track on the starboard tack, using tidal diamond B, for a period of one hour from 1300. Extend this ground track backwards to intersect with that of the port tack. Work out from the distance and speed made good on the port tack the ETA at the point of intersection. This is 1255. Similarly using the distance and speed made good on the starboard tack, the ETA at Poole Fairway buoy is **1329**.

HW Portsmouth is at 0740 BST and it is neap tides.

A3. 50°38'.2N 1°49'.4W

A4. 50°38'.9N 1°51'.1W

A5. Course to steer **265°M. ETA 1354.**

A6. Tidal Stream **353°T 0.9k.**
From the 1310 position plot the water track to obtain the DR position for 1355. The direction and distance of the 1355 fix from the 1355 DR position is the tidal stream experienced. Note that the 1355 fix used the bearing of the buoy *from* the yacht. The actual tidal stream on a passage is usually slightly different from that predicted from tidal diamonds which are calculated for the exact position of the diamond.

A.7 Course to steer **248°M. ETA 1418**. Measure the bearing of Poole Fairway buoy from the anchorage (073°M) and approach the anchorage maintaining a course to keep the buoy steady on that bearing. If an object or a transit can be identified ahead on the shoreline, then use that instead.

A8. Least depth of water (at next LW) 3.5m. Length of anchor cable: **18m if all chain, or 26m** if a combination of chain and nylon warp. The bottom is **fine sand (fs)**.

	Time	LW Height	HW Height	LW Height	Range
Portsmouth	1210 GMT	1.8	4.0	1.6	2.2
Differences	– 0105	– 0.5	– 2.3	– 0.7	neaps
Swanage	1105 GMT	1.1	1.7	0.9	
Add 1 hour	+ 0100				
Swanage	1205 BST				

1420 is LW + 2h 15m: height of tide is 1.4m
Charted depth = 4.0 – 1.4 = 2.6m
Depth of water at next LW = 0.9 + 2.6 = 3.5m
Depth of water at next HW = 1.7 + 2.6 = 4.3
Length of chain = 4 × max. depth = 4 × 4.3 = 17.2m
Length of chain plus warp = 6 × max. depth = 6 × 4.3 = 25.8m

CHAPTER NINETEEN

19.1a.   A stopper knot, such as a figure of eight.
   b.   A round turn and two half hitches.
   c.   A bowline.

19.2a.   Nylon because of its strength and shock absorbing qualities.
   b.   Polyester, because it is strong with low stretching properties.
   c.   Polypropylene, because it is buoyant.

19.3   A bowline which is used to make a temporary loop in a line.

19.4   Bow and stern lines; bow and stern spring lines; and bow and stern breast lines.

19.5   To keep your fingers clear of the winch drum to avoid getting them trapped and causing an injury.

CHAPTER TWENTY

20.1   a. To stop the boat yawing in a strong wind, when the boat is windrode. Both anchors will be laid from the bows with an angle between them of 40 degrees.
   b. To reduce the swinging circle of a boat in a strong tidal stream when there is not much wind. Both anchors will be laid from the bows, the heavier in the direction from which the strongest tidal stream is expected. The second in the opposite direction.

20.2   *Fisherman's anchor;*
   1. can be stowed flat.
   2. Few moving parts to trap the fingers.
   3. Heavier anchor required to give the same holding power as a CQR anchor.
   4. Anchor chain may get fouled on the vertical fluke when the anchor is on the seabed.

CQR anchor:
   1. Cannot be stowed flat.
   2. Movable parts which can trap fingers.
   3. Lighter anchor required to give the same holding power as a fisherman's anchor.
   4. Digs in well unless the point becomes impaled.

20.3   A trip line is used if the anchor is likely to become fouled on an obstruction. The trip line is used to haul up the anchor by the crown.

20.4a.   Good holding ground free from obstructions.
   b.   Maximum shelter from all expected wind directions.
   c.   Out of strong tidal streams.

d. Clear of other boats at all states of the tide.

e. A position where the boat does not ground and where there is sufficient anchor chain for the maximum expected depth.

f. Out of busy areas.

g. Where there are suitable transits or landmarks for bearings to check the boat's position.

h. If going ashore, near a suitable landing place.

20.5a. By exhibiting a ball as high as possible in the fore part of the boat.

b. By exhibiting an all-round white light as high as possible in the forepart of the boat.

CHAPTER TWENTY-ONE

21.1 In rough weather, especially when on deck, at night, and when alone in the cockpit. The safety line should be clipped to a strong point on the boat.

21.2 Shout 'man overboard' to alert crew and throw in the dan buoy to mark the position.

21.3a. No smoking below deck.

b. Engine compartment and bilges cleaned and ventilated regularly.

c. Gas bottles installed outside in the cockpit where any leaks drain overboard and not into the bilges.

d. Gas should be burned out of pipes after cooker is used and gas turned off at the bottle.

e. Engine checked regularly for oil and fuel leaks.

f.   Hatches should be closed when fuelling and the boat well ventilated afterwards. If there is any spillage this should be hosed down.

g. The correct up-to-date fire appliances should be carried in readily accessible positions.

21.4 2 red parachute rockets, 2 red handflares, 2 handheld orange smoke flares.

21.5 MAYDAY MAYDAY MAYDAY
This is MOTOR BOAT JETTO JETTO JETTO
MAYDAY MOTOR BOAT JETTO
My position is 3 miles south-west of Needles lighthouse
I am sinking and require immediate assistance
I have 4 persons on board
OVER

CHAPTER TWENTY-TWO

22.1   Keep a good look out.

22.2a.   Make a large enough alteration of course to be immediately apparent to the other boat.
   b.   Make the alteration in good time.
   c.   Make the alteration with due regard to the observance of good seamanship.

22.3a.   Neither. Both must alter course to starboard.
   b.   B has right of way, A should go astern of B.
   c.   B has right of way as she is in starboard tack. A should bear away or go astern of B or tack.

22.4a.   When she is overtaking boat.
   b.   When the motor boat is hampered in any way and cannot manoeuvre freely.
   c.   When the motor boat, because of its draught, cannot navigate outside a deep draught channel.

22.5   By taking repeated compass bearings of the approaching boat. If the bearing does not appreciably alter then a risk of collision is deemed to exist.

CHAPTER TWENTY-THREE

23.1

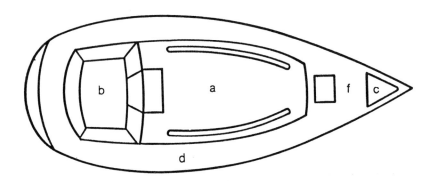

23.2

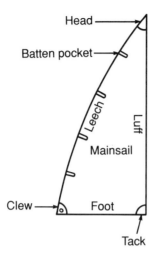

Head ———→

Batten pocket ——→

Leech

Luff

Mainsail

Clew ——→   Foot

Tack

23.3a. Movement through the water stem first.
  b. With heavy following seas the boat can slew round uncontrollably, heeling dangerously.
  c. An area in which a vessel can navigate without difficulty or danger of hitting an obstruction.
  d. A boat that heels easily is said to be tender, the opposite of stiff. The boat's 'dinghy; is sometimes referred to as her 'tender'.
  e. The breadth of a boat. The direction at right angles to the fore-and-aft line.

23.4 Official notice issued weekly or at other times detailing corrections to charts and hydrographic publications.

23.5 A zinc plate fastened to the hull to prevent corrosion of metal fittings on the hull.

TEST PAPER B

B1. HW Dover 1000 GMT or 1100 BST. 1300 BST is HW + 2. Range = 5.9 − 1.6 = 4.3m which is just under half way from neaps to springs (see Mean Ranges on Fig 7.1). From Fig 8.1 for 2 hours after HW at Dover (HW + 2), off Anvil Point the tidal stream would appear to be 2.3 knots at springs and 1.3 knots at neaps. At 1300 BST on 22 August the tidal stream is likely to be between 1.7 and 1.8 knots in the direction 250°(T).

B2.   From extract 1, on 18 May in Dover Low Water is at 0925 GMT with a height of tide of 1.2m. 1025 BST is equivalent to 0925 GMT, so the height of tide at 1025 BST is 1.2m above chart datum. Depth of water $= 1.2 + 1.5 = 2.7$m.

B3.   a. 'B', the overtaking boat, gives way by altering course to port.
b. 'B', on port tack, must be prepared to give way if she cannot determine on which tack 'A' is sailing: stand by to go about. Being on the same tack, 'A' as windward boat gives way going astern of 'B'. This is an instance where it is important to take positive action in ample time.
c. 'B' has right of way as she is constrained by her draught. She should maintain her course and speed.

B4.   a. East cardinal.
b. To port.
c. Q(3) 10s.

B5.   a. Bowline.
b. Sheet bend.
c. Round turn and two half-hitches.
d. Figure of eight.
e. Sheet bend.

B6.   a. Side lights, stern light and steaming light.
b. Side lights, stern light and steaming light.
c. Tri-colour light *or* side lights and stern light.
d. White all-round light preferably in fore part of vessel (clipped to forestay).

B7.   a. Pre-stretched polyester (terylene).
b. Polyester (terylene).
c. Polypropylene.
d. Nylon.

B8.   One prolonged blast followed by two short blasts at intervals not exceeding 2 minutes.

B9.   1. Gun or other explosive signal fired at one minute intervals.
2. Continuous sounding of fog-signalling apparatus.
3. Red rocket parachute flare.
4. The morse Code signal . . . – – – . . . (SOS) by light or sound.
5. The radiotelephony signal MAYDAY.
6. International Code signal N C.
7. A signal consisting of a square flag above or below a ball.
8. Flames on the vessel.
9. Red hand flare.
10. A smoke signal giving off orange coloured smoke.

11. Slowly and repeatedly raising and lowering arms outstretched to each side.

12. Signals transmitted by emergency position-indicating radio beacons (EPIRBs).

B10.   MAYDAY MAYDAY MAYDAY
This is YACHT DABBLER, YACHT DABBLER, YACHT DABBLER,
MAYDAY YACHT DABBLER
My position is 180 degrees from ANVIL POINT distance 2 miles
I have struck an underwater object and I am in danger of sinking
There are 4 adults and 1 infant on board
I require immediate assistance
OVER

B11.   Beaufort force 5.

B12.   a. From 15 to 25 knots.
b. Less than 2 miles.
c. From 6 to 12 hours.

B13.   a. 153°(M).
b. 001°(M).
c. 358°(M).

B14.   Yellow.

B15.   4° 09'W.

Extract 1

Lat. 51°07'N. Long. 1°19'E.

DOVER

HIGH & LOW WATER

MAY

	Time	m		Time	m
1	0036	6.4	**16**	0017	6.4
	0757	0.9		0745	0.8
F	1300	6.2	Sa	1248	6.4
	2006	1.1		2008	0.9
2	0107	6.2	**17**	0109	6.3
	0827	1.1		0833	0.9
Sa	1331	6.0	Su	1341	6.2
	2042	1.3		2057	1.0
3	0137	5.9	**18**	0206	6.0
	0901	1.4		0925	1.2
Su	1405	5.8	M	1434	6.0
	2118	1.4		2152	1.2
4	0212	5.5	**19**	0307	5.8
	0938	1.7		1026	1.5
M	1447	5.5	Tu	1531	5.8
	2159	1.9		2257	1.4
5	0301	5.2	**20**	0414	5.6
	1020	2.1		1136	1.6
Tu	1545	5.2	W	1637	5.6
	2249	2.1			
6	0419	4.9	**21**	0010	1.5
	1115	2.3		0539	5.5
W	1701	5.1	Th	1250	1.6
	2354	2.2		1800	5.5
7	0550	4.8	**22**	0127	1.4
	1227	2.4		0659	5.6
Th	1817	5.1	F	1404	1.5
				1914	5.7

JUNE

	Time	m		Time	m
1	0120	5.8	**16**	0208	6.2
	0840	1.4		0934	1.0
M	1348	5.9	Tu	1426	6.3
	2101	1.5		2159	0.9
2	0157	5.6	**17**	0300	6.1
	0915	1.6		1028	1.2
Tu	1427	5.8	W	1517	6.1
	2141	1.7		2254	1.1
3	0242	5.4	**18**	0356	5.9
	0955	1.8		1123	1.4
W	1515	5.6	Th	1612	5.9
	2224	1.8		2353	1.2
4	0342	5.2	**19**	0459	5.7
	1041	2.0		1221	1.5
Th	1614	5.5	F	1716	5.8
	2318	1.9			
5	0452	5.1	**20**	0055	1.4
	1136	2.1		0608	5.6
F	1719	5.4	Sa	1323	1.7
				1824	5.8
6	0021	1.9	**21**	0201	1.5
	0557	5.2		0712	5.6
Sa	1243	2.1	Su	1426	1.7
	1819	5.5		1928	5.8
7	0127	1.8	**22**	0305	1.5
	0653	5.4		0809	5.7
Su	1349	2.0	M	1525	1.7
	1914	5.7		2026	5.9

JULY

	Time	m		Time	m
1	0138	5.9	**16**	0237	6.3
	0857	1.5		1013	1.0
W	1405	6.1	Th	1450	6.4
	2121	1.4		2235	0.9
2	0219	5.7	**17**	0324	6.1
	0929	1.6		1052	1.3
Th	1444	6.0	F	1539	6.2
	2159	1.5		2319	1.2
3	0305	5.6	**18**	0416	5.9
	1006	1.8		1134	1.6
F	1531	5.8	Sa	1633	6.0
	2240	1.7			
4	0400	5.5	**19**	0008	1.5
	1049	1.9		0516	5.6
Sa	1624	5.7	Su	1224	1.9
	2329	1.8		1737	5.7
5	0458	5.4	**20**	0107	1.8
	1143	2.1		0627	5.6
Su	1720	5.7	M	1328	2.1
				1850	5.6
6	0028	1.8	**21**	0219	2.0
	0557	5.4		0737	5.4
M	1248	2.1	Tu	1443	2.1
	1819	5.7		2001	5.6
7	0133	1.8	**22**	0327	2.0
	0657	5.5		0839	5.6
Tu	1359	2.1	W	1546	2.0
	1920	5.7		2101	5.6

AUGUST

	Time	m		Time	m
1	0223	5.9	**16**	0335	5.9
	0934	1.6		1040	1.7
Sa	1442	6.1	Su	1552	6.0
	2202	1.5		2313	1.7
2	0304	5.7	**17**	0431	5.5
	1010	1.8		1122	2.1
Su	1524	5.9	M	1654	5.6
	2244	1.7			
3	0356	5.5	**18**	0005	2.2
	1055	2.0		0546	5.2
M	1620	5.7	Tu	1225	2.4
	2337	1.9		1819	5.2
4	0459	5.4	**19**	0126	2.4
	1158	2.2		0710	5.2
Tu	1727	5.5	W	1359	2.5
				1944	5.2
5	0046	2.0	**20**	0254	2.4
	0612	5.3		0820	5.3
W	1319	2.2	Th	1524	2.2
	1845	5.4		2051	5.4
6	0206	2.0	**21**	0357	2.1
	0740	5.4		0917	5.6
Th	1449	2.0	F	1620	1.9
	2009	5.6		2145	5.6
7	0332	1.7	**22**	0447	1.8
	0903	5.7		1000	5.9
F	1614	1.6	Sa	1705	1.6
	2124	5.8		2224	5.8

WHEN TO ENTER — The best time is between −0200 and +0100 (Dover).
WHEN TO LEAVE — All times suitable, but caution required when meeting stream off ent.
RATE AND SET — The stream in the entrance and harbour vary considerably. E. going stream begins −0210 (Dover). Sets 068°, 4 knots (Springs), 2½ knots (Neaps). W. going stream begins +0430 (Dover). Sets 224°. 2½ knots (Springs), 1½ knots (Neaps).

Extract 2

TIDAL DIFFERENCES ON DOVER

PLACE	TIME DIFFERENCES				HEIGHT DIFFERENCES (Metres)			
	High Water		Low Water		MHWS	MHWN	MLWN	MLWS
DOVER	0000 and 1200	0600 and 1800	0100 and 1300	0700 and 1900	6.7	5.3	2.0	0.8
Hastings	0000	−0010	−0030	−0030	+0.8	+0.5	+0.1	−0.1
Rye (Approaches)	+0005	−0010	—	—	+1.0	+0.7	—	—
Rye (Harbour)	+0005	−0010	—	—	−1.4	−1.7	Dries	Dries
Dungeness	−0010	−0015	−0020	−0010	+1.0	+0.6	+0.4	+0.1
Folkestone	−0020	−0005	−0010	−0010	+0.4	+0.4	0.0	−0.1
Deal	+0010	+0020	+0010	+0005	−0.6	−0.3	0.0	0.0
Richborough	+0015	+0015	+0030	+0030	−3.4	−2.6	−1.7	−0.7
Ramsgate	+0020	+0020	−0007	−0007	−1.8	−1.5	−0.8	−0.4

NOTE: Rye should be carefully considered. It dries out, tidal streams are strong and rough weather can make Rye Bay very dangerous for small vessels.
Folkestone is unsuitable except in emergency.
Ramsgate is an excellent harbour for all small yachts.

Extract 3

PORTSMOUTH

HIGH & LOW WATER   **GMT** ADD 1 HOUR MARCH 29 — OCTOBER 25 FOR B.S.T.

MAY

Day	TIME	M	Day	TIME	M
1 F	0059	4.5	**16** SA	0047	4.7
	0610	0.8		0606	0.6
	1327	4.4		1320	4.5
	1827			1829	0.9
2 SA	0131	4.4	**17** SU	0132	4.5
	0642	0.9		0653	0.7
	1403	4.2		1413	4.4
	1858	1.3		1917	1.1
3 SU	0203	4.2	**18** M	0222	4.3
	0717	1.2		0744	0.9
	1441	4.1		1510	4.3
	1937	1.6		2012	1.4
4 M	0240	4.0	**19** TU	0319	4.1
	0800	1.5		0843	1.1
	1524	3.9		1616	4.2
	2026	1.9		2119	1.6
5 TU	0327	3.7	**20** W	0425	3.9
	0852	2.1		0953	1.3
	1620	3.7		1729	4.1
	2132	2.1		2237	1.7
6 W	0430	3.5	**21** TH	0544	3.8
	1000	1.9		1112	1.4
	1732	3.6		1845	4.1
	2254	2.1		2357	1.6
7 TH	0549	3.4	**22** F	0702	3.8
	1122	1.9		1226	1.3
	1848	3.6		1951	4.2
8 F	0013	1.9	**23** SA	0104	1.4
	0707	3.5		0807	4.0
	1234	1.7		1327	1.2
	1952	3.8		2043	4.3
9 SA	0113	1.7	**24** SU	0158	1.2
	0808	3.7		0859	4.1
	1329	1.4		1417	1.1
	2039	4.1		2127	4.4
10 SU	0158	1.4	**25** M	0242	1.1
	0855	4.0		0944	4.3
	1413	1.1		1500	1.0
	2121	4.3		2207	4.5
11 M	0238	1.1	**26** TU	0322	0.9
	0935	4.3		1026	4.4
	1454	0.9		1542	1.0
	2201	4.6		2245	4.6

JUNE

Day	TIME	M	Day	TIME	M
1 M	0143	4.1	**16** TU	0213	4.4
	0659	1.2		0739	0.8
	1423	4.1		1503	4.5
	1919	1.6		2007	1.3
2 TU	0220	4.0	**17** W	0307	4.3
	0738	1.3		0834	1.0
	1504	4.0		1602	4.5
	2004	1.7		2105	1.4
3 W	0302	3.8	**18** TH	0407	4.1
	0822	1.5		0934	1.1
	1550	3.9		1703	4.4
	2055	1.8		2209	1.5
4 TH	0352	3.7	**19** F	0512	4.0
	0916	1.6		1039	1.3
	1642	3.9		1807	4.2
	2155	1.9		2318	1.6
5 F	0451	3.6	**20** SA	0623	3.9
	1017	1.6		1147	1.4
	1741	3.8		1909	4.2
	2301	1.8			
6 SA	0557	1.6	**21** SU	0025	1.5
	1123	1.6		0732	3.9
	1843	3.9		1252	1.4
				2006	4.2
7 SU	0005	1.7	**22** M	0125	1.4
	0702	3.8		0832	4.0
	1227	1.5		1349	1.4
	1939	4.1		2055	4.2
8 M	0101	1.5	**23** TU	0217	1.3
	0800	4.0		0924	4.1
	1323	1.3		1437	1.4
	2031	4.3		2141	4.3
9 TU	0153	1.3	**24** W	0303	1.2
	0854	4.2		1011	4.2
	1416	1.1		1523	1.3
	2122	4.5		2223	4.4
10 W	0241	1.0	**25** TH	0345	1.1
	0946	4.4		1055	4.3
	1506	1.0		1604	1.3
	2211	4.6		2303	4.4
11 TH	0330	0.9	**26** F	0425	1.1
	1038	4.5		1136	4.3
	1556	0.9		1643	1.2
	○ 2300	4.7		● 2341	4.3

JULY

Day	TIME	M	Day	TIME	M
1 W	0203	4.0	**16** TH	0248	4.5
	0719	1.1		0815	0.8
	1442	4.2		1535	4.7
	1941	1.5		2041	1.3
2 TH	0240	4.0	**17** F	0338	4.4
	0756	1.2		0905	1.0
	1520	4.2		1626	4.5
	2021	1.5		2133	1.4
3 F	0320	3.9	**18** SA	0434	4.1
	0837	1.3		1000	1.3
	1600	4.1		1721	4.3
	2106	1.6		2233	1.6
4 SA	0404	3.9	**19** SU	0538	3.9
	0925	1.4		1104	1.6
	1647	4.0		1820	4.1
	2159	1.7		2341	1.7
5 SU	0458	3.8	**20** M	0651	3.8
	1023	1.5		1214	1.7
	1740	4.0		1925	4.0
	2300	1.7			
6 M	0602	3.8	**21** TU	0052	1.7
	1130	1.6		0805	3.8
	1842	4.0		1323	1.8
				2026	4.0
7 TU	0009	1.6	**22** W	0157	1.6
	0712	3.9		0910	3.9
	1239	1.5		1423	1.7
	1947	4.2		2121	4.1
8 W	0116	1.4	**23** TH	0250	1.5
	0821	4.1		1003	4.0
	1345	1.4		1512	1.6
	2051	4.3		2210	4.1
9 TH	0218	1.2	**24** F	0336	1.3
	0927	4.3		1047	4.2
	1447	1.2		1555	1.4
	2151	4.5		2252	4.2
10 F	0317	1.0	**25** SA	0415	1.2
	1027	4.6		1125	4.3
	1543	1.0		1632	1.3
	2247	4.6		● 2329	4.3
11 SA	0411	0.8	**26** SU	0450	1.1
	1123	4.6		1200	4.3
	1636	0.9		1708	1.2
	○ 2339	4.6			

AUGUST

Day	TIME	M	Day	TIME	M
1 SA	0251	4.1	**16** SU	0356	4.2
	0806	1.0		0919	1.4
	1525	4.3		1630	4.3
	2027	1.3		2147	1.6
2 SU	0330	4.1	**17** M	0452	3.9
	0847	1.2		1017	1.8
	1604	4.2		1727	4.0
	2112	1.5		2254	1.8
3 M	0416	3.9	**18** TU	0607	3.7
	0937	1.5		1133	2.1
	1653	4.0		1838	3.8
	2211	1.6			
4 TU	0518	3.8	**19** W	0017	2.0
	1045	1.7		0737	3.6
	1800	3.9		1259	2.1
	2328	1.7		1958	3.7
5 W	0640	3.8	**20** TH	0138	1.9
	1210	1.8		0854	3.7
	1917	4.0		1411	1.9
				2106	3.8
6 TH	0052	1.6	**21** F	0239	1.7
	0806	3.9		0951	3.9
	1331	1.6		1503	1.7
	2034	4.1		2158	4.0
7 F	0208	1.4	**22** SA	0325	1.4
	0919	4.1		1033	4.1
	1439	1.3		1544	1.4
	2140	4.3		2239	4.2
8 SA	0311	1.0	**23** SU	0400	1.2
	1021	4.4		1106	4.3
	1538	1.1		1618	1.3
	2239	4.5		2312	4.3
9 SU	0406	0.8	**24** M	0432	1.0
	1115	4.6		1136	4.4
	1629	0.9		1649	1.1
	○ 2329	4.6		● 2343	4.3
10 M	0454	0.6	**25** TU	0502	0.9
	1205	4.8		1205	4.4
	1717	0.8		1721	1.0
11 TU	0015	4.7	**26** W	0011	4.3
	0540	0.5		0534	0.8
	1251	4.9		1236	4.5
	1802	0.8		1753	1.0

Extract 4   **TIDAL DIFFERENCES ON PORTSMOUTH**

PLACE	TIME DIFFERENCES				HEIGHT DIFFERENCES (Metres)			
	High Water		Low Water		MHWS	MHWN	MLWN	MLWS
PORTSMOUTH	**0000** and **1200**	**0600** and **1800**	**0500** and **1700**	**1100** and **2300**	**4.7**	**3.8**	**1.8**	**0.6**
Swanage	−0250	+0105	−0105	−0105	−2.7	−2.2	−0.7	−0.3
Bournemouth	−0240	+0055	−0050	−0030	−2.7	−2.2	−0.8	−0.3
Christchurch (Entrance)	−0230	+0030	−0035	−0035	−2.9	−2.4	−1.2	−0.2
Christchurch (Tuckton)	−0205	+0110	+0110	+0105	−3.0	−2.5	−1.0	+0.1
Hurst Point	−0115	−0005	−0030	−0025	−2.0	−1.5	−0.5	−0.1
Lymington	−0110	+0005	−0020	−0020	−1.7	−1.2	−0.5	−0.1
Bucklers Hard	−0040	−0010	+0010	−0010	−1.0	−0.8	−0.2	−0.3
Stansore Point	−0050	−0010	−0005	−0010	−0.9	−0.6	−0.2	0.0
Isle of Wight								
Yarmouth	−0105	+0005	−0025	−0030	−1.6	−1.3	−0.4	0.0
Totland Bay	−0130	−0045	−0040	−0040	−2.0	−1.5	−0.5	−0.1
Freshwater	−0210	+0025	−0040	−0020	−2.1	−1.5	−0.4	0.0
Ventnor	−0025	−0030	−0025	−0030	−0.8	−0.6	−0.2	+0.2
Sandown	0000	+0005	+0010	+0025	−0.6	−0.5	−0.2	0.0
Foreland	−0010	0000	+0005	+0010	−0.4	−0.4	−0.3	−0.2
Bembridge Harbour ...	−0010	+0005	+0020	0000	−1.6	−1.5	−1.4	−0.6
Ryde	−0010	+0010	−0005	−0010	−0.2	−0.1	0.0	+0.1
Medina River								
Cowes	−0015	+0015	0000	−0020	−0.5	−0.3	−0.1	0.0
Folly Inn	−0015	+0015	0000	−0020	−0.6	−0.4	−0.1	+0.2
Newport	−	−	−	−	−0.6	−0.4	+0.1	+1.3
PORTSMOUTH	**0500** and **1700**	**1000** and **2200**	**0000** and **1200**	**0600** and **1800**	**4.7**	**3.8**	**1.8**	**0.6**
Lee-on-the-Solent	−0005	+0005	−0015	−0010	−0.2	−0.1	+0.1	+0.2
Chichester Harbour								
Entrance	−0010	+0005	+0015	+0020	+0.2	+0.2	0.0	+0.1
Northney	+0010	+0015	+0015	+0025	+0.2	0.0	−0.2	−0.3
Bosham	0000	+0010	−	−	+0.2	+0.1	−	−
Itchenor	−0005	+0005	+0005	+0025	+0.1	0.0	−0.2	−0.2
Dell Quay	+0005	+0015	−	−	+0.2	+0.1	−	−
Selsey Bill	−0005	−0005	+0035	+0035	+0.6	+0.6	0.0	0.0
Nab Tower	+0015	0000	+0015	+0015	−0.2	0.0	+0.2	0.0

The first H.W. of spring tides is shown.

Extract 5

TO FIND DISTANCE OFF LIGHTS RISING OR DIPPING

Height of Light		HEIGHT OF EYE											
		Metres											
		1.5	3	4.6	6.1	7.6	9.1	10.7	12.2	13.7	15.2	16.8	18.3	19.8
		Feet											
		5	10	15	20	25	30	35	40	45	50	55	60	65
m	ft													
12	40	9¾	11	11¾	12½	13	13½	14	14½	15	15½	15¾	16¼	16½
15	50	10¾	11¾	12½	13¼	14	14½	15	15½	15¾	16¼	16¾	17	17½
18	60	11½	12½	13½	14	14¾	15¼	15¾	16¼	16½	17	17½	17¾	18¼
21	70	12¼	13¼	14	14¾	15½	16	16½	17	17¼	17¾	18	18½	19
24	80	13	14	14¾	15½	16	16½	17	17½	18	18½	18¾	19¼	19½
27	90	13½	14½	15½	16	16¾	17¼	17¾	18¼	18½	19	19½	19¾	20¼
30	100	14	15	16	16½	17¼	17¾	18¼	18¾	19¼	19½	20	20½	20¾
34	110	14½	15¾	16½	17¼	17¾	18¼	19	19¼	19¾	20¼	20½	21	21¼
37	120	15¼	16¼	17	17¾	18¼	19	19½	20	20¼	20¾	21	21½	22
40	130	15¾	16¾	17½	18¼	19	19½	20	20½	20¾	21¼	21½	22	22½
43	140	16¼	17¼	18	18¾	19½	20	20½	21	21¼	21¾	22	22½	23
46	150	16¾	17¾	18½	19¼	19¾	20½	21	21¼	21¾	22¼	22½	23	23¼
49	160	17	18¼	19	19¾	20¼	20¾	21½	21¾	22¼	22¾	23	23½	23¾
52	170	17½	18½	19½	20	20¾	21¼	21¾	22¼	22¾	23	23½	24	24¼

Extract 6

ANVIL POINT 50°35.5'N, 1°57.5'W. Lt. Fl. 10 sec. 24M. vis. 237° to 076°. White Tr. 45m. Horn(3) 30 sec. shown H24.
PEVERIL LEDGE By. Can. R. Off Peveril Pt.

SWANAGE
Pier Lt. 2 F.R. vert. 3M. White mast with lantern, 6m. on N arm of Pier.

POOLE 50°41'N 1°56'W. Tel: Poole (0202) 685261 (Night: Broadstone 692149)
Pilotage: E.T.A. required 12 h and 2 h in advance.
P/Station: Radio—Cutter cruises near Poole Bar By. when required.
Radio—Port: VHF Chan. 16, 14. Hours 0900-1700 Mon.-Fri.
Radio—Pilots: VHF Chan. 16, 14, 9, 6—Cont.
Poole Hbr. Y.C. Marina (0202) 707321. Chan. M. Apr.-Oct. 0800-1600.
Entry Signals: Floating breakwater of tyres showing 6 in. above water between Fishermans Dock breakwater and centre dolphin opp. Town Quay. Vessels navigating between Little Channel, Fishermans Dock and E end of Town Quay should not pass between centre of E Dolphins and W end of Fishermans Dock breakwater.
Lifting Bridge between Poole Town and Lower Hamworthy.
R.Lt.—do not approach bridge (vessels entitled to request bridge to be opened contact Poole Bridge on VHF Chan. 14.)
Do not pass Stakes Lt. By. until distant signal observed.
Bridge opening times: Mon.-Fri. 0930, 1130, 1430, 1630, 1830, 2130, 2330; Sat.-Sun. & Bank Hol. 0730, 0930, 1130, 1330, 1530, 1730, 1930, 2130.
Sandbanks Ferry when working displays 1 B. ball or W., G., R. Lts. vert. Ferry gives way to other vessels in Harbour. Sound 4 short blasts for ferry to keep clear. Allow enough time for ferry to manoeuvre.

SWASH CHANNEL

POOLE FAIRWAY Lt.By. L.Fl. 10 sec. Pillar R.W.V.S. Topmark Sph. Bell.
TRAINING BANK Lt.Bn. Q.R. 2M. R.Tr. 7m. marks seaward end of training wall on SW side of Swash Channel. 10 stakes with R. Can. Topmarks at intervals along Training Bank.

Bar No: 1 Lt.By. Q.G. Conical G. Bell.
No: 3 By. Conical G.
No: 5 By. Conical G.
No: 7 By. Conical G.
No: 9 By. Conical G.
No: 11 By. Conical G.
HOOK SANDS No: 13 Lt.By. Fl.G. 3 sec. Conical G.
HOOK SANDS Bn. B.Y. Topmark N.
No: 15 By. Conical G.
No: 17 By. Conical G.
No: 19 By. Conical G.

No: 2 Lt.By. Fl.(2)R. 10 sec. Can.R.
No: 4 By. Can R.
No: 6 Punch & Judy By. Can. R.
No: 8 By. Can. R.
No: 10 By. Can. R.
No: 12 Channel Lt.By. Fl.R. 3 sec. Can. R. W of centre inner end Swash Channel.
No: 14 By. Can. R.
No: 16 By. Can. R.

SOUTH HAVEN POINT. Sandbanks Ferry Lts. Q.R. Ferry Landing.
NORTH HAVEN POINT. W of Haven Hotel (Conspicuous).
SAND BANKS. Lt.Bn. F.Or. 10M. vis. 315°-135° 4m. R.C.
FERRY LANDING. Lt. 2 F.G. vert. on W side of Ramp. (When approaching signal 4 long blasts.)

continued

Extract 6 *continued*

EAST LOOE CHANNEL

EAST LOOE Lt.By. Q.R. Can. R. marks E Looe Chan.
EAST HOOK By. Can. R. marks E. side Hook Sands.
EAST LOOE Lt.Bn. Oc.W.R.G. 6 sec. W.10M., R.6M., G.6M. Col. 9m. R.234°-294°;
W.294°-304°; G.304°-024°.

N. HAVEN POINT. Lt.Bn. Q.(9) 15 sec. Topmark W.
3 Cable Bns. Lt.F. between N Haven Pt. and Brownsea Castle.
18a Lt.By. Fl.(2)R. 5 sec. Can. R.
No. 18 Lt.By. Fl.R. 5 sec. Can. R.

POOLE TO NEEDLES CHANNEL

POOLE HEAD By. Can. Y. marks sewer off Poole Head.
BRANKSOME CHINE By. Can. Y. marks sewer off Branksome.
ALUM CHINE By. Can. Y. marks pipes off Alum Chine.
WHITBREAD MARK YACHT RACING By. Can.Y.

BOURNEMOUTH 50°43'N, 1°52'W. Tel: Bournemouth 28282.
Entry Signals: R. flag or R. Lt. at Bournemouth or Boscombe Pier at half mast—vessels must not go
alongside.

PIER HEAD. 2 F.R. vert. 2m. apart, white post with lantern, 8m. 1M. Reed(2) 120 sec. when ships
expected. Also bell to assist steamers.
BOURNEMOUTH PIER OUTFALL. By. Can. Y. marks drain pipes near Pier.

BOSCOMBE 50°43'N, 1°50'W
PIER HEAD. 2 F.R. vert. on R. Col. 7m. 1M. F.R.Lts. on hotel shown 289.5°, 0.51M. from Pier Lt.
BOSCOMBE PIER OUTFALL. By. Can. Y.

CHRISTCHURCH 50°47'N, 1°50'W
Air Lt. Al.Fl.W.G. 10 sec. at Hurn Aerodrome.
CHRISTCHURCH LEDGE By. Pillar Y.B. Topmark S.
CHRISTCHURCH BAY WAVE RESEARCH. Struct.Lt.Bn. Mo(U) 15 sec. Mo(U) R. 15 sec. 8m. Horn
Mo(U) 30 sec.
N HEAD.50°42.6'N, 01°35.4'W Lt.By. Fl.(3)G. 10 sec. Conical G. marks W end N Chan. apprs. to
the W Solent.

Extract 7

JULY

G.M.T.   **(31 days)**   **G.M.T.**

☉ SUN ☉

DATE			Equation of Time		Transit	Semi-diam.	Lat. 52°N.				Lat. Corr. to Sunrise, Sunset, etc.				
Day of			0 h.	12 h.			Twilight	Sunrise	Sunset	Twilight	Lat.	Twilight	Sunrise	Sunset	Twilight
Yr.	Mth.	Week													
			m. s.	m. s.	h. m.		h. m.	h. m.	h. m.	h. m.	°	h. m.	h. m.	h. m.	h. m.
182	1	W	+03 38	+03 44	12 04	15.8	02 55	03 44	20 23	21 12	N70	S.A.H.	S.A.H.	S.A.H.	S.A.H.
183	2	Th	+03 50	+03 55	12 04	15.8	02 56	03 44	20 23	21 12	68	S.A.H.	S.A.H.	S.A.H.	S.A.H.
184	3	F	+04 01	+04 07	12 04	15.8	02 57	03 45	20 23	21 11	66	T.A.N.	-2 21	+2 19	T.A.N.
185	4	Sa	+04 12	+04 18	12 04	15.8	02 58	03 46	20 22	21 10	64	T.A.N.	-1 42	+1 40	T.A.N.
186	5	Sun	+04 23	+04 28	12 04	15.8	02 59	03 47	20 22	21 10	62	-2 21	-1 14	+1 14	+2 21
187	6	M	+04 34	+04 39	12 04	15.8	03 00	03 48	20 21	21 09	N60	-1 27	-0 54	+0 54	+1 27
188	7	Tu	+04 44	+04 49	12 05	15.8	03 01	03 49	20 20	21 08	58	-0 55	-0 37	+0 37	+0 56
189	8	W	+04 53	+04 58	12 05	15.8	03 03	03 50	20 20	21 07	56	-0 33	-0 22	+0 23	+0 34
190	9	Th	+05 03	+05 07	12 05	15.8	03 04	03 51	20 19	21 06	54	-0 15	-0 10	+0 11	+0 15
191	10	F	+05 12	+05 16	12 05	15.8	03 05	03 52	20 18	21 05	50	+0 13	+0 10	-0 10	-0 13
192	11	Sa	+05 20	+05 24	12 05	15.8	03 07	03 53	20 18	21 04	N45	+0 39	+0 30	-0 30	-0 39
193	12	Sun	+05 28	+05 32	12 06	15.8	03 08	03 54	20 17	21 03	40	+0 59	+0 46	-0 46	-0 59
194	13	M	+05 36	+05 39	12 06	15.8	03 09	03 55	20 16	21 02	35	+1 16	+1 00	-0 59	-1 16
195	14	Tu	+05 43	+05 46	12 06	15.8	03 11	03 56	20 15	21 00	30	+1 30	+1 12	-1 11	-1 30
196	15	W	+05 50	+05 53	12 06	15.8	03 12	03 57	20 14	20 59	20	+1 53	+1 32	-1 31	-1 52
197	16	Th	+05 56	+05 59	12 06	15.8	03 13	03 58	20 13	20 58	N10	+2 12	+1 46	-1 48	-2 11
198	17	F	+06 02	+06 04	12 06	15.8	03 15	04 00	20 12	20 56	0	+2 28	+2 05	-2 04	-2 27
199	18	Sa	+06 07	+06 09	12 06	15.8	03 16	04 01	20 11	20 55	S10	+2 43	+2 21	-2 19	-2 43
200	19	Sun	+06 12	+06 14	12 06	15.8	03 17	04 02	20 10	20 54	20	+2 59	+2 38	-2 36	-2 59
201	20	M	+06 16	+06 18	12 06	15.8	03 19	04 04	20 08	20 52	30	+3 15	+2 57	-2 54	-3 15
202	21	Tu	+06 19	+06 21	12 06	15.8	03 20	04 05	20 07	20 51	S35	+3 25	+3 08	-3 06	-3 25
203	22	W	+06 23	+06 24	12 06	15.8	03 22	04 06	20 06	20 50	40	+3 35	+3 21	-3 18	-3 35
204	23	Th	+06 25	+06 26	12 06	15.8	03 24	04 08	20 04	20 48	45	+3 38	+3 36	-3 33	-3 47
205	24	F	+06 27	+06 26	12 06	15.8	03 25	04 09	20 03	20 46	S50	+4 02	+3 55	-3 51	-4 02
206	25	Sa	+06 29	+06 29	12 06	15.8	03 27	04 10	20 02	20 45					
207	26	Sun	+06 29	+06 30	12 06	15.8	03 29	04 12	20 00	20 43					
208	27	M	+06 30	+06 30	12 06	15.8	03 30	04 13	19 58	20 41					
209	28	Tu	+06 29	+06 29	12 06	15.8	03 32	04 15	19 57	20 40					
210	29	W	+06 28	+06 28	12 06	15.8	03 34	04 17	19 55	20 38					
211	30	Th	+06 27	+06 26	12 06	15.8	03 35	04 18	19 54	20 36					
212	31	F	+06 25	+06 23	12 06	15.8	03 37	04 19	19 53	20 34					

For longitude west, add 4 minutes per degree.
For longitude east, subtract 4 minutes per degree.

Extract 8 **Beaufort Wind Scale**

Beaufort Number	Mean Wind Speed in Knots	Description	Sea State
0	Less than 1	Calm	Sea like a mirror.
1	1-3	Light air	Ripples with the appearance of scales are formed but without foam crests
2	4-6	Light breeze	Small wavelets, still short but more pronounced. Crests have a glassy appearance and do not break.
3	7-10	Gentle breeze	Large wavelets. Crests begin to break. Foam of glassy appearance Perhaps scattered white horses.
4	11-16	Moderate breeze	Small waves becoming larger. Fairly frequent white horses.
5	17-21	Fresh breeze	Moderate waves taking a more pronounced long form. Many white horses are formed. Chance of some spray.
6	22-27	Strong breeze	Large waves begin to form; the white foam crests are more extensive everywhere. Probably some spray.
7	28-33	Near gale	Sea heaps up and white foam from breaking waves begins to be blown in streaks along the direction of the wind.
8	34-40	Gale	Moderately high waves of greater length; edges of crests begin to break into spindrift. The foam is blown in well-marked streaks along the direction of the wind.

Index

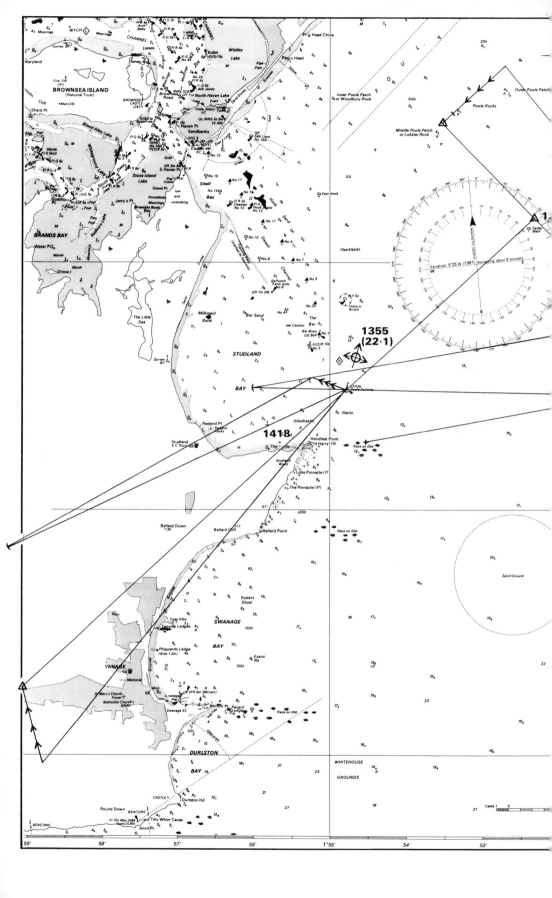

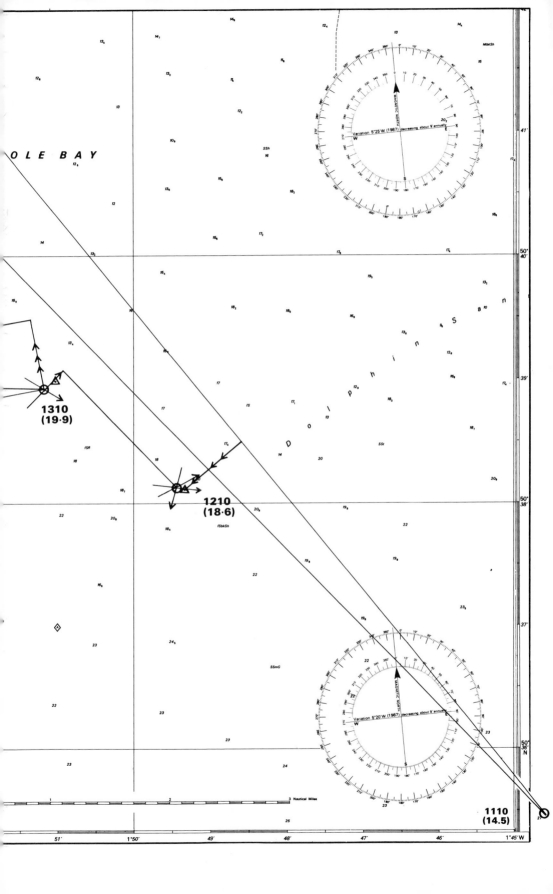

The Parlour Song Book

Also available in Pan Books
PARLOUR POETRY

CONDITIONS OF SALE